D0760386

Tank force: Allied armor in World War II

Kenneth Macksey

Editor-in-Chief: Barrie Pitt
Art Director: Peter Dunbar

Military Consultant: Sir Basil Liddell Hart
Picture Editor: Bobby Hunt

Executive Editor: David Mason
Designer: Sarah Kingham
Special Drawings: John Batchelor
Cartographer: Richard Natkiel
Cover: Denis Piper
Research Assistant: Yvonne Marsh

Contents

Lack of faith

Introduction by Lieutenant-General Sir Charles Broad

In this interesting, even enthralling book, Kenneth Macksey makes the unpreparedness of Britain, France and America for the late war abundantly clear. This lack of readiness is a chronic disease with democracies and Britain in particular has always suffered from it. She was as unready for the War in the Crimea as for the Boer War and the First World War; but why should she have been so for the Second World War, since she had been first in the field with the tank?

By the autumn of 1914 the thick belts of barbed wire in front of the German trenches had become the chief obstacle to Allied infantry attack, for the amount of artillery available at that time to the British and French was insufficient to cut lanes through them, and thus the tank was originally conceived by the French and British as a sort of armoured steam roller to make passages through the barbed wire. Later on in the war, when the artillery had increased enormously in number, calibre and effectiveness, the barrage cut the wire, and forced the defenders to take cover in their dug-outs thus enabling the attacking infantry to enter their trenches.

But machine-guns had also increased in numbers, and inevitably some were missed by the barrage, and one was enough to do great damage.

I have seen 100 or more men lying in a row, cut down by one machine-gun although the rest of the attack was successful and the machine-gun eventually scuppered.

This, of course, led to the dispersal of the available tanks to attack infantry companies, as immediate assistance against machine-guns was required if the infantry were not to fall behind the barrage. Nevertheless at Cambrai on 20th November 1917, 476 tanks, led by Brigadier Hugh Elles in person and flying a flag made by his wife, showed what could be achieved when used in mass at the right time and place.

I was then an artillery man and I visited the battlefield at Cambrai the next day. It was remarkable for the undisturbed nature of the ground, for the few dead lying about, and for the success achieved compared with those on the Somme battlefields or on the appalling desolation of Passchendaele.

The first few years after the war were spent by the few visionaries of the time in a fight to preserve tanks in the armies of France, Britain and America; but it was from Britain that the lead came.

In 1926 General Sir George Milne came to the British War Office as Chief of the Imperial General Staff with a determination to modernise and mechanise the army; and he

collected a team of young colonels, mostly from the Tank Corps and with myself among them, to help him. Our hopes were high in those days that the British Army was about to be modernised in a similar fashion to that in which the Royal Navy had been brought up to date before the First World War by Admiral Fisher.

But it was not to be. Milne did not have quite the faith to act decisively, and it was difficult to blame him. It would have been a drastic step to take in those days, and was one that all the leading generals in Europe refused to take. Only a politician, Hitler, took the plunge, and he was though by the soldiers to be a gambler at best – even perhaps to be mad! Thus it was that the Germans alone profited by the British work, as General Guderian himself has said.

In 1938 I was senior umpire on an exercise in Britain when the tanks were mainly old and in small numbers, while the anti-tank guns were represented by green flags waved by the umpires and jocularly known as the dominant arm! I was accosted by the German Military Attaché and told I ought to come clean, instead of keeping everything hidden; he simply didn't believe that we were as defenceless as we seemed to be.

In the ensuing pages, Kenneth Macksey tells the story of the Allied defeats and of the German successes: the one due mainly to faulty preparation for war, and the other to correct application of known principles – it was as simple as that. We learn how France suffered 'total defeat and Britain nearly the same fate, owing to lack of leaders trained for modern war. We also see how Britain remained always one step behind in technology, and how the intervention of America with an army and a mass of machines redressed the balance. We find that in America, too, the initial resistance to the tank idea was as inflexible as elsewhere. The story of tank forces is thus of a struggle to introduce new ideas against old-fashioned opposition.

Throughout this book runs the theme of another classical struggle: that between guns and armour, together with the attempt to keep tanks within manageable limits of size, balanced against the need to increase protection and striking power. These are the everlasting problems which not only dominated tanks forces in the Second World War but also dominate them in the present day.

The reader should be provoked into relating this lucid description of the past to the resolution of problems in the future.

The struggle for recognition

It was typical of all its perversity that the First World War – a war which had generated a violent tactical stalemate and slaughter on a vaster scale than had ever been known before – should have ended before the tank, the principal cause of its tactical solution, had been tested to certainty. For three years, from 1914 to the end of 1917, the armies of the Central Powers and the Allies had remained locked in struggle along a belt of land that was little more than twenty miles wide though several hundred miles in length between the North Sea and the Swiss frontier, held in place by impenetrable, wired-in, entrenched fortifications. During those three deadlocked years all manner of means to restore open and decisive combat had been tried – from increasingly heavy bombardments with high explosive to progressively more insidious paralysis by the use of poison gas. But only one land weapon in the end showed that, in conjunction with others, it held the secret of the combination to unlock battle-fronts. That weapon was the armoured fighting vehicle – better known as the tank – driven by a petrol engine, carried on caterpillar tracks, protected by bullet and splinter proof plate and armed with machine-guns and cannon.

Tanks, working in co-operation with infantry, artillery and, to a lesser extent, aircraft, revolutionised warfare in just two years of hectic development. Since the first British machines tentatively explored their possibilities at the Battle of Flers-Courcellette on 15th September 1916, to the initial use by the French of their own tanks on the Chemin des Dames on 16th April 1917, then through the frustrating, muddy shambles of Passchendaele until the triumphant vindication of the first massed tank attack at Cambrai on 20th November 1917, the men who believed in armoured fighting vehicles had to fight their own authorities for the chance to use the new weapons with almost the same vigour as they wished to fight the real enemy. And even after Cambrai, where tanks led infantry in tearing a five mile hole in the German lines, a struggle for recognition still went on because the victory was not complete and a strong body of military leaders continued to doubt the ability of armoured vehicles to break the enemy lines and in addition inflict a total defeat by exploitation – the role, until then, sedulously reserved for the traditional pursuit force, horsed cavalry. Only after a tactically skilful German offensive (lacking tanks in quantity) had dominated the war from March to July 1918 and been defeated because flesh and blood – men and horses – had failed to exploit a clean break-through, could the Allies return to the offensive. Tanks had played a limited, though at times crucial role in stopping the German advance. At Amiens on 8th August 1918, over 400 British tanks rolled across the German defences to herald a rain of blows by successive British, French and American attacks, nearly all led by tanks. In three months those blows were to help bring the war to a sudden end.

Nevertheless the breaching of the German lines was never complete. Pursuit of their retreating armies was inevitably conditioned by the slow pace of the tanks of the day, by their inherent unreliability and their short range of action. Success was tainted by set-backs, for whenever tanks broke through cavalry failed, in the face of machine-guns, to profit from the break and at the same time, tank casualties became extremely heavy in the face of well-directed German artillery fire. It was significant, however, that tank casualties were in inverse proportion to the numbers engaged: tanks in mass suffered fewer losses than tanks in small numbers – largely because tanks could only be destroyed by direct, aimed fire and enemy gunners shot straighter the less they were distracted by a proliferation of targets. The Allies understood this but, for

shortage of machines, were not often able to take advantage of it, and the war was over before enough tanks were available to carry out the dictum of the French tank leader, General Jean Estienne, of 'offensive action in mass and by surprise'.

French tanks had different design characteristics from the British, for the majority of French tanks were small two-man Renault FTs of 1917, whereas the British machines were either the large eight-man, rhomboidal version or the smaller three-man Medium 'A' (or Whippet). But in tactical doctrine there was little variation and the technique of close co-operation between tanks and infantry was faithfully copied by the Americans who, for want of a tank of their own design and manufacture, had to make do with British and French types. Tanks simply accompanied infantry behind an artillery barrage directed against known enemy positions. Having reached those positions they proceeded to demolish them and destroy the enemy. If, after that, the faster medium tanks, in company with horsed cavalry, could maintain the momentum of the advance, so much the better, but only rarely did this happen and therefore penetrations of the enemy lines seldom exceeded five miles before a halt had to be called when the tanks broke down or ran out of fuel. To remedy this failure British designers tried to build medium sized tanks with greater range and speed, improved reliability and superior combat worthiness. From the battle front they were urged on by the leaders of the British Tank Corps under Brigadier Hugh Elles, but it was Elles' GSO I, Colonel J F C Fuller, who laid down the master plan which, if the war had gone into 1919, would have ordered the employment of tanks. Looking into the near future, Fuller wrote 'Plan 1919' – which he described as a novelette but which, in fact, was the blue print for all future tank tactics.

Fuller argued that by placing a man

General S D Rockenbach, US Tank
Corps commandant

Colonel J B Estienne – father of
French tanks

'. . . in a bullet proof petrol-driven car, he is able to concentrate the whole of his muscular energy on the manipulation of his weapons'. He went on to point out that '. . . the potential fighting strength of a body of men lies in its organisation' and that one way to destroy an organisation was '. . . the rendering inoperative of its power of command – brain warfare'. Armoured cross-country vehicles, he argued, could move freely '. . . over the open, irrespective of roads and without the limiting factor of animal endurance'. He showed how, since 1914, very few attacks had penetrated as far as the enemy artillery positions, and none had got as far as the enemy headquarters which were the centres of control and communication. He went on to say that fast moving columns of medium tanks, finding and entering a gap in the enemy defences by day or night, could drive deep into the enemy lines making straight for headquarters and supply centres. Ahead would go aircraft to bomb and further disturb enemy composure and thought. Then, as the enemy fell into confusion, a conventional attack by heavy tanks supported by artillery and infantry would be launched along a ninety mile front in what Fuller called, 'a morcel-lated attack', in which the tanks concentrated overwhelmingly against selected points and then fanned out behind the front – once it had been broken – catching the surviving enemy in flank and rear, and pursuing him to destruction with armoured cars, mechanised artillery and lorried infantry. If all went well, the enemy would be brought to the point of disruption, his main force broken into fragments, his leaders deprived of the means to give orders, his reserves paralysed for lack of information and direction and his supplies in jeopardy.

But the war ended before a suitable medium tank could be made and before Plan 1919 could be tried out. It waited for another war, enshrined for all to read in Fuller's book, 'Memoirs of an Unconventional Soldier' – a foretaste of the future to be used by anybody who cared to make use of it.

Following five years unmitigated slaughter and dissipation of wealth, the nations could not be expected to spend much money on new military equipment when so much was left over from the war. For the armed services, be they of Germany, crushed and resentful under the restrictions imposed by the Versailles Treaty, or of Britain, France and America, redolent

Colonel J F C Fuller – the first tank genius

in the backwash of peace, the priorities lay heavily on the side of financial retrenchment commensurate with the necessity (in the case of the British and French) of policing the turbulent frontiers of their empires and of the Americans to escape into semi-isolation after their brief and traumatic emergence from behind the cover of the Monroe Doctrine. The British army, wedded to the Cardwell System which sent its best trained troops to India and other outposts and kept only a cadre to train recruits in Britain, could not bring itself to do more than experiment on the lines of Fuller's Plan 1919 – and it was declared War Office policy that expériments should be carried out as and when possible.

The French, torn between the need to maintain colonial forces and that of keeping a large, metropolitan conscript force for the purpose of retaining dominance over Germany, had more money to spare and far more tanks than any other army. For the majority of them the need to experiment seemed less important since they had won the war using an agreed formula in which the infantry had been the predominant factor. Tanks, like artillery, had been the servants

(and after 1920 an integral part) of the infantry because of the nature of warfare in which, to quote French General Staff *Provisional Instructions Concerning the Tactical Utilisation of Larger Units* of 1921, '. . . fire power had given a remarkable strength of resistance to improvised fortifications'. Thus, according to the French, attack fell into disrepute and could only take place '. . . in favourable conditions after the assembly of powerful material means, artillery, tanks, munitions, etc. . .' when tanks '. . . make it easier for the infantry to proceed by smashing the passive obstacles and the active resistance offered by the enemy'. There was more in similar tone, a tone which ignored the pleas of a minority led by Estienne who spoke in favour of a mechanised force of 100,000 men in tanks, carriers and artillery carriers.

It was the misfortune of the US Tank Corps that in 1919, when its future was in the melting pot, its commandant, Brigadier-General S D Rockenbach, was not prepared to argue for more than maintenance of the *status quo*. Convinced as he was that there was a need for a tank corps separate in organisation from the infantry, he nevertheless could project his imagination no further than the concept of tanks working as an adjunct to infantry at infantry pace. The scope of Plan 1919's grandeur eluded him, and he was overborne by pressure from General Pershing and others. In want of an influential advocate the Tank Corps was absorbed into the Infantry Corps in 1920 – a centralisation which dovetailed neatly with the economic outlook of Congress as expressed by one Congressman with, 'I am unable absolutely to see any reason during peacetime for the creation of the overhead that would have to be established to give you a separate organisation.' In response, Congress passed a budget for tanks in 1921 of only a paltry $79,000.

Under the stultifying dominance of

Left: Colonel G Patton with a Renault tank. *Above:* French St Chamonds
– just assault guns – move up. *Below:* The rivals – Australian horseman;
British tank in 1918

the Infantry Corps the American tank men did their best to survive, and by stunts and propaganda, to draw attention to their plight. The Tank School at Fort Meade ran a series of courses and demonstrations which tried to balance theory with practice, though the actual practice was inhibited by obsolete equipment and financial poverty. The Tank Corps Technical Board was disbanded in 1920 and not revived until 1924 when it reappeared under the title of the Tank Board; until then there was almost a standstill in the recommendation of new equipment and techniques and of practical trials, but thereafter the Board, working with the approval of the Chief of Infantry, was enabled to make modest progress with new vehicles, armaments, communications system and methods. They could not show much in hardware but at least, without being

Left: Renault and infantry under fire. *Below:* Dawn of a new era – British Mark Vs crawl into action near Amiens in 1918

'heretical', they were creating something upon which a later generation could build if need be.

Heresy was being effectively preached elsewhere, however, and the devil incarnate was Fuller who, encouraged by the War Office policy of experiment, was writing a prolific series of internal departmental minutes and external propaganda in the military journals, setting out the future of warfare in the way he saw it, being governed by armoured mechanisation. After Fuller came others to intensify the literary bombardment. In America an article of mild and orthodox content by a certain Captain Dwight D Eisenhower was officially condemned by his superiors, whereupon he declined to burst into print in public again for many years; a more virulent and far sighted article by Colonel George Patton (who, unlike Eisenhower, had active service experience of tanks in battle) suffered a similar fate.

Although Fuller was publicly condemned in Britain for his advocacy, he in no way recanted. Indeed he was rather surprised to receive profuse and paradoxical praise from the deputy chief of the French General Staff and to be honoured by the President of France with the award of the insignia and diploma of *Officier d'Academie* in recognition of a prizewinning essay setting out the clear philosophy and shape of war to come. However, while some French, along with every other foresighted military thinker throughout the world, gave a cheer, conservative British soldiers stood up to destroy the heretic in their midst, though fortunately Fuller was too strong for them. More fortunately still, he had managed, with the collaboration of others, to preserve the British Tank Corps in being and for this reason – and probably this alone – material progress with armoured formations was made in Britain during the twenties and early thirties when none was being made elsewhere.

A decade for experiment

The battle of the essays, which began in the early twenties when Fuller and his sympathisers opened the debate upon the future of war, only established a theoretical basis for practical, field experiments. Thoroughly practical experiments can be carried out properly only with realistic equipment which, if nothing else, simulates the actual thing. In 1920, when Fuller wrote his prize winning essay and Estienne was pleading for a mechanised army, there were still no tanks in existence which in any way resembled the machine with a speed of twenty miles an hour, a circuit of action of 150 to 200 miles and ability to cross a fourteen-foot gap and ordinary road or canal bridges, without breaking them down, such as Fuller had envisaged in Plan 1919. In 1919 the British Secretary of State for War, Mr Winston Churchill (to whom credit for the creation of tanks was due as much as to anybody) had made the best of an arbitrary ceiling to the military budget by laying down that every penny would have to be care-

fully spent and that the general approach to the future would be in the direction of experiments with new tactics to solve the problems left unsolved at the end of the war. There seemed no hurry, particularly since government policy proclaimed that 'the British Empire will not be involved in any great war during the next ten years, and that no Expeditionary Force will be required.' Under those conditions the British Army could only go on making do with its old, heavy wartime tanks with their maximum speed of five miles per hour, and with a few medium tanks capable of a speed no greater than eight miles per hour. The possibility of obtaining faster, modern tanks along with special cross-country carriers for infantry and artillery, to enable them to keep up with the tanks, was highly unlikely – and this perpetual state of financial stringency was to be the underlying reason for slow progress in mechanisation for several years to come.

It was also sensed by those in

authority that, if once the feasibility of a mechanised army was proved, almost every item of existing equipment in basically horse-drawn armies would be rendered obsolete overnight. The opposition to mechanisation by the die-hards of the cavalry, artillery and infantry in nearly all the armies of the world is readily understandable. It was not that the officers (and it had to be they who were most vociferous in their protests) wished to go to war on horseback – the realistic reticence of many to participate in charges against machine-gun fire in the First World War had been all too obvious – it was simply that the provision of official chargers gave them the benefit of free sport at the taxpayers' expense They would argue that to deprive the army of its horses would undermine the army of its attraction to future recruits, but ask many of the men what they thought and they would reply that the privilege of mucking out the horses was not worth the pleasure of living with the beasts; they would rather learn the modern motor trade and fit themselves for subsequent employment in a world that was becoming geared to the automobile.

Nevertheless the old guard in every nation would claim that the radical reorganisation which mechanisation would demand might unsettle an army's confidence but a short while after it had recovered from the upset of the greatest war in history. The majority of soldiers realised that mechanisation had to come, but those at the top had to tailor the demands of the progressives to fit in with the reactionaries and with the pace at which the politicians (who were at the beck and call of pacifist voters) and financiers would allow re-equipment to take place. It was therefore to the credit of the British Army Council, prodded hard by the Tank Corps, that it actually sanctioned the purchase of over 160 brand new, fast tanks in 1924 when other armies were quite content to make do with wartime machines.

And although the tank the British bought, the Vickers Medium Mark I, was hardly battleworthy since its 6.5mm armour could barely stop bullets, in other important respects it went far to satisfy Fuller's specifications, for it had a speed of eighteen miles per hour, a range of 150 miles and carried both machine-guns and an anti-tank cannon in a fully rotating turret. It was thus suitable as a tactical test bed which, when joined in the mid-twenties by a handful of tracked infantry and artillery carriers, became the centre-piece of the nucleus of a fully mechanised cross-country force.

Despite the signing of the Treaty of Locarno in 1925, and the atmosphere of peace and goodwill it engendered, and after many false starts, a small armoured force came into being in the summer of 1927 and was known as the Experimental or Mechanised Force or Formation. It was composed of:-

3rd Bn Royal Tank Corps – the reconnaissance unit, equipped with twenty armoured cars and eight armoured carriers;

5th Bn Royal Tank Corps – the main striking element, equipped with forty nine medium tanks of which four carried radio for communication with Force HQ;

2nd Bn Somerset Light Infantry – for protection of the tanks, equipped with Vickers machine-guns and carried in half tracked or six wheeled lorries;

9th Field Brigade Royal Artillery – to provide fire support, equipped with eighteen pounder guns towed by tracked Dragons, carried in half tracked or on self-propelled chassis, and

9th Light Battery – equipped with 3.7-inch howitzers on half tracks; 17th Field Company Royal Engineers – to help cross obstacles and clear routes, carrying its equipment on six wheeled lorries;

Various squadrons of the Royal Air Force to provide intimate close support, fighter protection and longer range bombing of the enemy.

The Force contained every important element of every armoured formation of the future with the exception of specialised vehicles for crossing gaps and clearing minefields. Of little more than brigade strength, it was nevertheless self-sufficient, even though its endurance in protracted operations would have been short-lived – but then this force was gathered together for trial only and not for battle. Its deficiencies in other respects were no less apparent, for while every vehicle had some kind of cross-country capability, the tracked elements were bound to leave the wheeled elements far behind over fields, while the wheeled elements were faster and badly matched to the tracks when travelling in column of march on the roads. Orders had to be given at the halt, and fresh plans – to take advantage of the fluctuations of highly mobile conditions in which the situation could change momentarily – could only be passed, after a prolonged delay, by messengers. The Commander, an infantry officer with no previous experience of mechanised forces (and not Fuller who had declined the post after a disagreement over his terms of reference) reacted cautiously and slowly since he thought of operations moving at slow infantry pace and of delivering ponderous blows on a broad front when, in fact, the force was capable of moving thirty miles a day and drew its killing power from an ability to pierce the enemy lines like a stiletto. For all this a profound impression was made and never more than when, in the concluding phases of the exercises after the various ill-mixed components had settled down into their prescribed roles, the Force was pitted against a conventional horse and foot army.

The conventional army was invited to advance thirty miles and occupy high ground. The Mechanised Force, positioned eighty miles off, was told to frustrate and dislocate the conventional army. And so it did, for the conventional army could never feel safe while fast moving armoured cars raced round their flanks to attack them in rear when out-pacing horsed cavalry vedettes had utterly failed to give warning of the hostile approach. Deprived of information from its traditional source – the slow moving cavalry patrols – the main foot army dared not move except in short terrified bursts from one so-called tank-proof locality to another – in other words from village to village and copse to copse. Even then they were frequently caught by surprise in the open and driven into disorder until, gradually, the conventional army began to disintegrate in the face of a greatly superior though numerically inferior enemy. Small local checks at the front caused the main marching columns in rear to concertina and these in turn presented close packed columns to detection and 'bombardment' from the air. Then, when confusion had reached its height, at dusk one evening, the rabble was attacked by tanks and could make no coherent response. Eventually the conventional army found it could move only by night, but so slow was its progress and so easily was its route plotted by the mobile forces, that a system of ambush and blocking positions, set up by the Mechanised Force across its predicted path, stopped all further manoeuvre. At the end of the exercise the cavalry and infantry were in check, still only half way to their objective, and the exercise ended with a resounding victory for the Mechanised Force.

The experiment was more far reaching in terms of world-wide propaganda than in any other respect. In 1928, when the British Force was given another outing before final disbandment, the US Army assembled its own mechanised force at Fort Meade in Maryland, but since its tanks were only slow and very unreliable First World War heavies (of British derivation) and lights (of the

Renault type) there could be no attempt at sweeping manoeuvres such as the British were practising with their fast mediums. This force was disbanded after a predetermined period. Of equal significance in the USA that year was the appearance of a striking prototype tank designed by J Walter Christie, an engineer who had made a study of armoured warfare and who was convinced that the future of war would be conditioned by very fast armoured vehicles which were capable of an unassisted crossing of almost every conceivable obstacle. Christie's 1928 tank was certainly faster than any seen before, though its armour and armament were very poor, but the vehicle was also hamstrung by defects in the revolutionary suspension and track design. Nevertheless, even though insufficient time and effort had gone into engineering development, the shape of the future was there to be seen and this was not the last to be heard of Christie.

The three years following 1928 marked a pause in major experiments. This was hardly surprising since not only had the progressives to gather their thoughts and persuade their conservative superiors to allow another adventure into the unknown, but the ravages of the worst economic collapse in history had been met by fierce retrenchment in the armed services of almost every nation. This contraction was, of course, highly commendable to those who strove for disarmament and who were preparing for a forthcoming Disarmament Conference. Experiments in mechanisation were bound to take second place when military leaders were fighting for the very survival of their Services. The French, British and American armies had suffered the resignation of many of their best officers and men throughout the

French D1 – a reluctant horse for the new armoured Cavalry Brigade

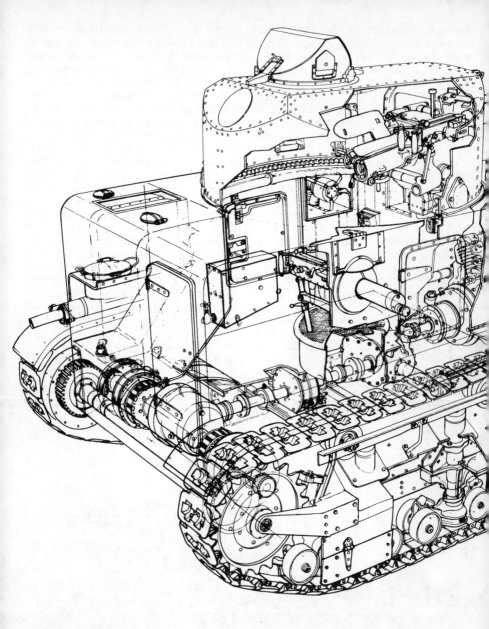

Britain's best bet for tactical trials. The unbattleworthy Vickers Medium
Mark II whose meagre 6.5mm armour plate was hardly bullet proof
Weight: 13 tons. *Armament:* 1 × 47mm and 6mgs. *Speed:* 18mph
Range: 120 miles. *Crew:* 5

twenties. Discouraged by the lack of purpose and future offered by their seemingly decaying profession, they turned to other work. The British Army, with its pay cut by ten percent, was 8,000 men under strength in 1931, when unemployment was at its height and the Ten Year Rule still held good.

In 1931 the American Army had reached its nadir at a strength of only 134,000 and the Chief of Staff, General Douglas MacArthur, was heard to plead with Congress in 1932 (after he had disbanded yet another Experimental Armoured Force) 'They suffer tremendously from one thing and one thing only – that Congress will not give them enough money to equip them properly with modern tanks.' Nevertheless, MacArthur was infected by the same doubts as his contemporaries with regard to tanks, seeing them either as a substitute for horses or as an adjunct to infantry, but not as an element for decision in their own right. Faced with the choice of spending limited money on manpower or tanks he not unexpectedly opted for the former.

In 1929 the British had published their findings as the result of the 1927/8 experiment – a little booklet entitled, 'Mechanized and Armoured Formations' – better known as the Purple Primer since, between its purple covers, it set-out to teach the fundamental lessons associated with the new brand of warfare. In a lucid, modern style it covered a wide range of future possibilities, bearing in mind the pamphlet's own injunction that '. . . changes in equipment are constantly occurring, and each improvement brings in its train consequent changes in tactics and organisation'. Every type of existing armoured and unarmoured mechanical vehicle was analysed and then related to the organisations to which they might be fitted and the tactics that might be employed. A positive distinction was made between Combat and Mobile troops – and this

Above: General Douglas MacArthur had reservations about the value of tanks. *Right:* US Cavalry's combat car – Christie's T3 of 1931

was most important since it confirmed the doctrine (inherent in Plan 1919) that one type of formation was required for close fighting and another quite different one for open warfare, just as infantry had once been needed for the former activity and horsed cavalry for the latter. Light armoured divisions were envisaged which 'In certain terrain . . . will be capable of acting independently of cavalry and infantry' and there was still a role foreseen for the horseman '. . . in areas where the power of the horse to move over difficult ground can be exploited' – but this, as Fuller would have said, was to propitiate the horse-worshippers.

To the organisers the establishment tables printed at the back of the book gave essential precedents and data when they came to form the next experimental force – and this took place in 1931 when a complete armoured brigade of medium and light tanks was gathered together on Salisbury Plain. The feasibility of mechanised forces was now accepted; each future move would be towards sophistication and the 1931 gathering had one aim set above all others – the

use of voice radio down to all tanks so that an entire force could be controlled by one man travelling in the midst of his command. Until 1931 only rabid enthusiasts had believed that a small voice radio could be successfully mounted in a tank. After the manoeuvres that summer, when Brigadier Charles Broad demonstrated how even the inefficient short range sets of the day gave him the power to pass tactical orders on the move, there could be no further doubts. To quote Liddell Hart, 'It presented a spectacle that had never before been seen – a mass of 180 tanks, marching and countermarching, wheeling and deploying, as a single body controlled by a single voice.'

After this success came the inevitable backlash from the reactionaries. Since infantry and artillery had been excluded from the experiment (for the good reason that its main purpose was to develop 'control' and not 'tactics') the infantrymen and gunners (who were also slowly developing their own mechanised vehicles) took the opportunity to revive fears that Broad and the Tank Corps were working towards

the creation of an All Tank Army, separate from the older Arms. These fears were transmitted to the 1931 edition of the Purple Primer (re-entitled 'Modern Formations') in which the Chief of the Imperial General Staff, Field-Marshal Sir George Milne, felt compelled to conclude, 'Though published by command of the Army Council, this pamphlet does not of necessity represent the considered views of that body, but is the result of five years' study by the General Staff.'

No matter how uncertain blew the trumpet in the British camp, the blast that had been given re-echoed strongly in Russia, in France and in America – and soon it would rever-berate in Germany where the tank enthusiasts in the tank-gelded post Versailles Treaty German army were laying their plans for the day when they became free from restrictions.

In America a second mixed Mechanised Force had been raised at Fort Eustis, Virginia, in 1930 and had included armoured cars manned by the cavalry as well as mechanised artil-lery. Though still equipped with obsolete machines plus a bewildering variety of experimental tanks, all of

different performance, this formation possessed staying power and survived until 1932. By then a wealth of useful experience had been accumulated, including knowledge of Christie's latest offering, the sleek T3 which, when tested by the Ordnance Board (which at that time included a Lieutenant-Colonel Adna Chaffee and Major George Patton) was found to be vastly superior to any of its pre-decessors. The most important out-come of the Fort Eustis experiment was an arrangement whereby the cavalry took over the development of mobile forces from the infantry and set up their own organisation at Fort Knox in Kentucky. Progress became no quicker as an immediate result of this diversification, but at least a new line of development was opened at a time when US Armour was in a state of atrophy. Moreover an element of competition was introduced since, from then on, the infantry would have to vie with the cavalry (not always to their mutual benefit) for new tanks, each suited to their particular purposes.

A somewhat similar reallocation of functions also took place in France at

23

about the same time. French cavalry had adopted armoured cars in addition to their horses as far back as 1914 (British cavalry did not take over armoured cars until 1927) and by 1930 a considerable measure of motorisation was altering the shape of the conventional cavalry divisions besides the reconnaissance element of infantry divisions. French progress was mostly empirical and inordinately slow, for the infantry and cavalry were loth to co-operate in the formation of a unified mechanised force, and, in addition, were extremely sceptical of British antics. Yet they had the means to copy the British had they so wished, since, although their basic tank remained the Renault FT, supplemented by a few experimental heavy tanks, the cross-country speed of the Renaults had been doubled by the substitution of more robust, sprung suspensions in place of the original rigid system. For French armour the year 1933 was critical, since then it took delivery of

its first D1 tanks (a considerable improvement on the modified Renaults) and included them in the first so-called Armoured Cavalry Brigade – a formation which owed its existence to the permission of General Weygand (Vice President of the Army Council who, like Milne and MacArthur, did not believe in them whole-heartedly) and which, in 1934, became known as the *Division Légère Mécanique* (DLM). For its day this was a remarkable formation because it comprised an admirably balanced force of all arms – better balanced in many ways than the embryonic German Panzer Divisions and, indeed, to many subsequent French and British armoured formations. As eventually composed it included:–
1. A reconnaissance regiment of forty armoured cars and two motor cycle companies;
2. Two regiments each of forty medium and forty light tanks;
3. Three motorised rifle battalions

each with twenty light tanks of their own;

4. A mechanised artillery regiment;

5. Engineers, transport companies and a squadron of reconnaissance aircraft.

Like every other emergent armoured force of the day, the DLM suffered severe trials and tribulations. Hamstrung by outmoded, horse-paced tactics they could draw on the experiences already propagated by the British, of course, but no amount of study or practice would compensate for the frailties of the D1 tank of which one report mentioned, 'thirty-one running, seventeen badly worn and sixty-two off the road.'

1933 was also the year in which the war clouds began to gather again as Hitler came to power and, as part of his programme of rearming the German army, started the creation of Panzer

Left: Broad controlling his brigade by radio. *Below:* Though some rely on flag signals

Divisions. The story is told in 'Panzer Division' (Weapon Book No 2 in the Ballantine Series) and will not be repeated here except to say that the ever darkening shadow cast by the German tank force from 1934 onwards threw increasing strains and doubts upon the military policies of France and Britain. The time available for experiments was running out. The next generation of tanks to leave the factory floors would have to take their place in organisations which, right or wrong, would go to war using the tentative tactics evolved in the mid-thirties.

Again the lead in organisational and tactical affairs came from Britain where the 1st Tank Brigade (fully established at last and no longer a conglomeration of units brought together for the occasion) held a series of exercises in 1934 which explored the problems of control and manoeuvre in much greater depth than had the exercises of 1931. Broad's place had

been taken by Brigadier Percy Hobart, an armoured enthusiast of great drive who had acted as GSO 1 to the Experimental Force during its last triumphant exercise against a conventional force in 1927 and had commanded a battalion of tanks during the 1931 exercises. In 1933 Hobart had written his scenario describing the armoured battle of the future:

'Caution will be rampant . . . We should play on the enemy's fears both by air and mobile force. Threats (or rumours even) of an armoured force in his rear, or near mobilisation centres at different places; probably little material damage (lorries here and there, detachments of troops etc) will be necessary or advisable. We must avoid losing tanks.

'When we have played on his nerves sufficiently, and when the preparations for our main strategic stroke are ready, then we strike in combination with all our forces. Tank thrust in this case will be at a vital point, and pushed really home. i.e. we must accept our losses.

'But here, as at all times, tank's true role is to ATTACK WEAKNESS. Use the Line of Least Resistance: Speed: Surprise.'

In his directive to the 1st Tank Brigade Hobart sought to examine and define every unknown aspect of control, supply, repair and recovery as well as co-operation with other Arms and with the Air Force. He envisaged the brigade being 'employed on a strategic or semi-independent mission against some important objective in the enemy rear . . . to induce the enemy to deploy in one direction and then to attack in another.' He did not reject the need to co-operate with mechanised infantry or artillery, as was frequently suggested, and this is emphasised by his proposals to take the next step into the unknown by combining, in one exercise, the operations of his tank brigade with armoured cars, an artillery regiment, and a mechanised infantry brigade. These proposals led to what has become known as the Battle of Hungerford in which the Mobile Force (nothing more nor less than the first armoured division ever) was pitted against a conventional army in a heavily simulated exercise in manoeuvre. But there was almost as much manoeuvring among the exercise directors and umpires as among the players, for the former had decided that the armoured enthusiasts needed curbing in order to help restore the morale of the older arms who were wilting beneath the evidence of their own impotence in face of the tank threat – and the Tank Corps' propaganda. Orders were given to the Mobile Force which circumscribed the alternative route approaches open to the tank brigade and which forced them to take unrealistic measures for which they were not designed. Even so the very suddenness of an advance by the Mobile Force still proved too quick for the umpires who (headed by Major-General Wavell) were no better at calculating tank speed than the larger part of the British Army: caught unawares, the umpires had to resort to unrealistic subterfuge in order to keep the exercise on its predetermined course. Provoked, but still in hand, the Mobile Force managed to maintain its cohesion, and when cut off from the rear, extricated itself in a daring night withdrawal which, again, baffled the exercise controllers.

On the surface (and to the chagrin of the armoured protagonists who were furious at being cheated) the Mobile Force seemed to have failed. In fact, it had proved the worth of its flexibility by its prompt and decisive reactions in the midst of appalling difficulties – difficulties such as would be multiplied by the uncertainties of real war.

As the exercise came to its end, staff officers in the British War Office took out formal proposals which had long ago been made by the Tank Corps for Mobile Divisions or, as they were to be called, Armoured Divisions. Thus, as the Germans laid down the framework of their first three Panzer Divisions,

the British and French tentatively set up one armoured division apiece. But at that point the future protagonists diverged in philosophy, for while the Germans were bent upon the creation of a strictly aggressive army in which Panzer Divisions were to be the weapon of decision capable of *all* phases of war, the French continued to believe in the ponderous viability of fixed fortifications and went on pouring milliards of francs and enormous quantities of material and labour into the construction of concrete and steel fortifications barring her frontier with Germany – and backed by a conventional army. And though Britain abandoned the Ten Year Rule in 1932 she by no means went the whole hog by committing herself to sending an expeditionary force to Europe in the event of war. Horrified at the prospect of another slaughter on the same scale as the First World War, the British hoped to be shielded by the French Army and the Maginot Line and to

Salisbury Plain: the brigade deploys 'as a single body controlled by one voice'

carry the war to the enemy through a naval and economic blockade and by air attack. For while the French believed that they might wear down the enemy on the Maginot Line prior to opening a long prepared offensive of their own, the British searched for panaceas in which material – in their case bombers working within the theory that 'they would always get through' – would win results with a minimum outlay in lives. In either case, French or British, armoured forces came second in order of priority when it came to the provision of money, men and machines – and they dropped to third priority when both nations opted for new infantry divisions on the same scale as in 1918, even though those divisions were to be more highly mechanised and therefore more mobile.

This then was the European scene in 1935 after the Germans had abrogated the Treaty of Versailles, reintroduced conscription and set the alarm bells ringing. In America there was little or no alarm, however, for isolation held the politicians and people in thrall and in the immediate aftermath of the Great Slump there was need to restore the economy. President Roosevelt, as Commander-in-Chief of the Armed Forces, could give them only cursory attention while he struggled to revitalise industry and cut down the number of unemployed. The strength of the Forces rose slightly, but the majority of the officers were getting too old for their jobs and not enough new ones were coming forward to replace them. Some battalions made do with only one officer and the number of technically inclined personnel was inordinately low. In 1932 the 7th Cavalry Brigade (Mechanised) came into being, but its existence was tenuous and its role governed strictly by the tenets of cavalry law which could only envisage horsemen acting as scouts or engaging in raids when the enemy was looking elsewhere. Tanks owned by the Infantry Corps continued to practise close co-operation in the deliberate assault on a broad front, but in America both the infantry and cavalry settled upon light tanks to do this work. They thought they were right to copy the French solution of 1918 and paid no heed to those who foresaw that improved light anti-tank guns in great numbers would massacre light tanks. But a divergence in design philosophy – between those who believed in the viability of light tanks and those who thought something heavier with thicker armour was necessary – lay at the heart of the debate surrounding the production of tanks – the same debate as marked the advent of tanks, which continued until the outbreak of war and which, indeed, continues to the present day.

Brigadier P C S Hobart with the new Medium

Expansion

When tanks were first introduced on to the battlefield in 1916 there were no properly established tactical doctrines to govern their behaviour. For some time the employment of tanks remained, to say the least, haphazard and at the whim of ignorance. Almost as much tactical foresight was evolved by the engineers who designed the tanks as by the soldiers who took them into action: in consequence the early designers tended strongly to make the tanks which they guessed the soldiers ought to have. But in the years succeeding the first post-war definitive experiments in Britain, the USA and on the Continent of Europe, the soldiers had acquired a wealth of practical experience and could give educated directions to the designers as to the kind of fighting vehicles they desired – desires which were commensurate with strategic plans, tactical doctrine and financial restrictions. And until Hitler came to power and restarted the Arms Race in 1933, the latter consideration was supreme. The purse strings were kept tightly closed to expensive mechanical devices so long as there seemed a chance of making old, First World War equipment last a little longer.

Thus British and French attempts to produce expensive, heavy tanks were invariably thwarted, and the British failed in their efforts to get permission to produce a greatly improved medium tank – the sixteen-ton A6 at a cost of £16,000 each – to replace the Vickers Medium, in the early thirties. Egged on by their Tank Corps (whose virility sprang as much from the challenge of sheer survival as a belief in armoured warfare) plus the experience gained in the mobile experiments, the British were forced to keep their minds open to the need for specific machines for specific work – and in the early thirties wanted:-

1. Fast, lightly armed and armoured tanks in quite large numbers to patrol the rugged frontiers of the

Empire and to act as a scouting and protection force to the main body of medium tanks in a future European or desert war;

2. Medium tanks, with heavier armour, a cannon and a speed not much lower than that of the light tank to perform as the central punch in the tank brigade, in European and desert war.

In fact the British envisaged swarms of light tanks (each weighing about five-tons and armed only with machine guns) advancing several miles to the front and flank of sixteen-ton medium tanks, in search of enemy opposition, with a view to directing the medium tanks – in company with infantry and supporting artillery – to either destroy, or find ways to side-step, the opposition and make for easier targets in the enemy rear. In due course they built both light tanks and cheaper medium tanks in addition to a special light armoured carrier, for use by infantry machine-gunners, plus a very heavily armoured, poorly armed and slow infantry support tank at a cost of £5,000. Thus the prime requirements of Plan 1919 were catered for – heavy tanks to make the break-through along with infantry on foot, helped by a few carriers, and light and medium tanks (also accompanied by infantry carriers) to exploit a rupture of the enemy lines (once it had been made) by driving deep and across the enemy communications. Nevertheless this was Plan 1919 upside down, since Fuller had envisaged penetration being followed by rupture and then exploitation; yet the ultimate aim was still likely to be achieved. More significant, from the vehicle design point of view, was confirmation of the need for two quite different types of battle tank (a slow heavy and a fast medium), the creation of large numbers of highly vulnerable light tanks, armed only with machine-guns which would be quite ineffective against enemy tanks, and of special infantry carriers. But the omission of tracked artillery carriers reduced the chance of artillery keeping up with a fast moving, cross-country tank and infantry carrier advance.

Within all armies there was controversy as to the best way to kill tanks. In the British Army the infantry believed that a portable, wheeled anti-tank gun, backed up by field artillery, would suffice. The British Tank Corps, on the other hand, believed in setting a thief to catch a thief and that tank versus tank battles would not only take place, but would be the best possible anti-tank method: this was their reason for mounting a special anti-tank gun in their medium tanks. The infantry therefore had to be prepared (without enthusiasm) to make do with the co-operation of the Infantry Tank Mark I which did not carry a cannon. And Mark I, with its slow speed and single machine-gun, was not only cramped by the strictures of economy (as already mentioned) but suffered from the uncertainties then inhabiting the mind of General Elles who, having won his reputation as commander of British tanks in the First World War and by the victory at Cambrai, had lost faith in the future of tanks since he believed they would be routed by modern anti-tank guns. Worse still, he happened to become Master General of Ordnance, and therefore responsible for tank procurement, just as rearmament got under way. It was only because he later became persuaded that 60mm of armour on the Mark I would resist penetration by the existing 47 and 37mm anti-tank guns that he allowed production to go ahead: other types of medium (or cruiser tanks as they were later called) his mind consigned to the scrap heap, while his power obstructed their procurement.

Something fundamentally similar happened to the French though the reason for their fateful tactical and tank design philosophy were different. Since they stuck to their empirical assumption, that offensive warfare was inconceivable, they had only to maintain short range, slow, well-

General Gamelin – saw the need for a weapon to beat the Panzers

General Weygand – lukewarm to further tank development

armoured infantry support tanks – decidedly better armoured and up-gunned versions of the Renault FTs, plus the good, heavy Char Bs. For cavalry reconnaissance they settled for lighter medium tanks – D1s, D2s and their successor, the twenty-ton Somua S 35 – all armed with the 47mm cannon. Meanwhile the DLM, the first one of which had come into being so encouragingly in 1933, failed to follow the British and German tactical example. By 1939 they were only three in number and were by no means considered as a decisive arm – a separate army as some cared to call it; instead they were just intended to cover the frontage of the field armies, if and when the Maginot Line was outflanked or pierced, and having completed that role they were to occupy positions from which they could either be parcelled out as mobile pill-boxes or gathered together as a mobile reserve for use as a rupture force if the enemy showed signs of breaking. For all his pro-motion of the first DLM, Weygand stood firm against further progress saying, 'Two armies – not at any price . . . We already have a mech-anized, motorized reserve. Nothing

need be created, everything exists.' His was the voice of reaction against Colonel Charles de Gaulle who, in 1934 (long after the other tank progressives had stated their case), published his little book, *Vers l'Armée le Metier,* in which the concept of armoured for-mations was advocated, though with nothing like the vehemence or pre-cision with which it had already been put forward by Fuller and his compatriots. Far weightier arguments came, however, from the President of the Army Council, General Gamelin, when, in October 1936, after the German remilitarisation of the Rhineland, he said, 'One must have implements to match the technique. The Germans have invented the Panzer Division, which is the tool of the sudden attack followed by exploitation in depth . . . We need an instrument stronger than the Panzer Division.' But the Army Council did not share his view and, in the nature of all Committees when faced with disagreements, referred the matter for further study – and did so again in 1938 as Austria crumbled, and would have put it off yet again had not the Munich crisis of September and the flagrant demonstration of fast, unopposed movement by Panzer

Colonel de Gaulle – wrote a book on the subject

Colonel Adna Chaffee – father of the United States armored force

Forces, disturbed their composure. Experiments were at last begun in December 1938 towards removal of the heavy Char B tanks from the infantry and their concentration, along with the lighter R and H 35 tanks into so-called *Divisions Cuirassée* (DCR) – a thoroughly ill-balanced formation composed of:–

1. Two regiments each of thirty 32-ton heavy Char B tanks – each armed with a 47mm and a 75mm gun;

2. Two regiments each of thirty-nine 12-ton light tanks – H 35s or 39s, armed with a 37mm gun;

3. A single battalion of motorised infantry;

4. Two artillery groups;

5. The usual engineer and transport services.

But by the time these had been considered in council there was insufficient time to reverse the defensive philosophy of the officers and change the training of the men at a moment when the French will to fight had been seriously eroded.

Outwardly the French reticence to make an armoured division, with genuinely offensive characteristics, was contradictory of official policy, for in 1936 *Instructions on the Tactical*

Utilisation of Larger Units had been diametrically altered. Now the crucial paragraph read, 'The offensive is the supreme form of action . . . Only the offensive allows definitive results to be obtained . . .' Probably the about turn came too late, for the Maginot Line was built – an edifice dedicated to static resistance – and, in any case, the French had suffered such cruel losses from the *offense à l'outrance* during the previous war that to invite them to repeat the experience was asking too much of a nation. The French army of 1939 was not the keen weapon of 1914 and, unfortunately for the French nation, the British Army was no better prepared than the French army to fight an armoured battle, while their future German opponent was as good as of old.

Despite their having taken the lead in experimentation, the British still did not possess a fully equipped armoured division as they reached the threshold of war in September 1939, and the only tanks which accompanied the British Expeditionary Force to France after Poland had been invaded and was being overrun by the German panzers, were a number of light tank regiments manned by the cavalry and

33

Left: Somua S35 – the staple
fighting vehicle of France's DLMs
Above: British Bren carrier Mark 1
– the infantry's contribution to
mechanised warfare

a single battalion of Mark I infantry
tanks. This feeble dilution of armour
had come about because of the insist-
ence of the British Army Council upon
adhering to the concept of an infantry
army. Slower than the German
and French armies to convert horsed
cavalry to mechanical fighting
vehicles, they had simultaneously deprived the Tank Corps of the priority
which would have maintained its
power as a dominant striking force.
Not until 1935 did the cavalry turn
seriously to manning light tanks and
then at a price, for the conversion of
men who had spent all their previous
service caring for horses not only put
a strain on their adaptability, but also
diverted members of the Royal Tank
Corps to instructing the newcomers

instead of improving their own skills.
It took time to teach a horse-man to
drive and to learn the desirability of
finding and rectifying faults on tanks
as they appeared in order to keep
refractory vehicles running. Meanwhile the argument as to whether a
mobile or armoured division was
needed at all waxed furiously in the
corridors of the War Office. And when
at last, in 1937, it was decided to form
a mobile division, a determined
attempt was made to deprive it of its
medium tank brigade (along with a
threat to scrap that brigade). This
would have left it composed only of
light tanks – light cavalry on tracks,
in fact, ready targets for a modern
Balaclava when called upon to charge
since that would be the only way they
could hope to get within striking distance of enemy tanks armed with
cannon when they themselves had
only machine-guns. Having finally
decided the argument in favour of
retaining the Tank Brigade within the

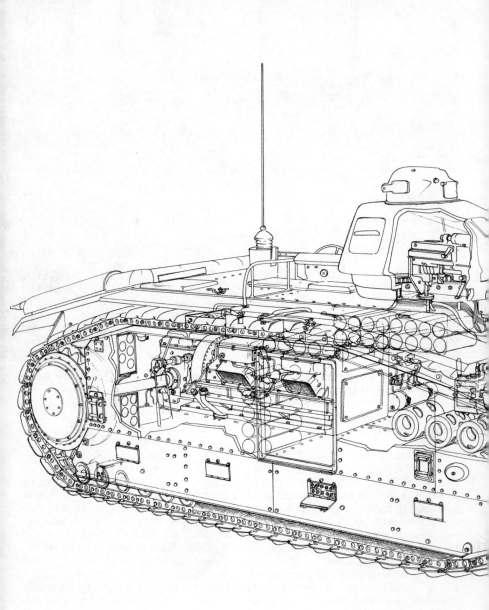

Main assault tank of the French tank forces but out of place in an armoured division because of its short 85-mile range. Char B's 60mm of armour was, however, proof against the 37mm anti-tank guns of 1940. *Weight:* 32 tons. *Armament:* 1 × 75mm, 1 × 47mm and 2mgs. *Speed:* 22mph. *Crew:* 4

Mobile Division, fresh indecision then arose as to who should command it, and since agreement could not be reached upon whether it should be a rather inadequate cavalry officer or a distinctly outspoken tank expert (Hobart) the job was given to an artilleryman (Major-General Brooke) who had been slow to take to mechanisation and had no experience of tanks.

As might have been expected, the organisation of the new division reflected the schism in concept, for while the cavalry had become committed to a future in armour alongside the Tank Corps, the British infantry had been much more reticent in keeping pace with progress, with the result that the role of reconnaissance and protection of the Tank Brigade, which could well have been undertaken by a brigade of armoured infantry (as in the French DLMs and German panzer divisions), was instead entrusted to armoured cavalry, the new division appearing in the following form:–

1. Two Cavalry Brigades each of three regiments of light tanks (reduced to one on the outbreak of war);

2. A Tank Brigade of one regiment of light and three of mixed light and medium tanks (converted to three regiments of medium tanks on the outbreak of war) and manned by the Royal Tank Corps;

3. Divisional troops (later called the Support Group) consisting of an armoured car regiment, two mechanical artillery regiments and two motorised infantry battalions (both the artillery and infantry reduced to one unit each on the outbreak of war).

Nevertheless these were the first steps to unity between the British Cavalry and Tank Corps which led to the formation of a single, Royal Armoured Corps on 1st April 1939.

Unlike the French, who possessed good, even if somewhat ill-conceived, tanks, the British had not one battleworthy tank at the time of the Munich crisis in 1938. Infantry tanks were in

course of production along with a great many light tanks, but the argument over the need for the cruiser and Elles' refusal to allocate sufficient money had resulted in appalling delays while cheap and (largely unavoidably) nasty designs were offered by the sole tank building firm of Vickers. Having been deprived of funds for research and development in an industry whose products demanded original technological knowledge, it could not be expected that immediately battleworthy and reliable vehicles would be manufactured overnight. Not until 1939 did the first new medium (or cruiser) tanks begin to appear off production – the Vickers thirteen-ton, A9 and A10 tanks armed with 40mm cannon, later to be followed by the much sleeker

Left: R-35 tanks – fellow travellers with French infantry, but strictly subordinate. *Below:* British cavalry convert to tanks – these are 9th Lancers in light Mark VIBs

looking Nuffield cruiser A13. The former were poor compromises, the latter a great step forward (though riddled with teething troubles), the result of an expansion in the tank building world when Nuffields were persuaded to purchase one of Walter Christie's fast tanks in order to re-design and re-engineer it into a practical, battleworthy tank. It was hardly their fault that, lacking experience, they got some details wrong.

The tanks which were to meet head-on in the first year of war began to concentrate behind the frontiers in August 1939 as the Germans signed their non-aggression pact with Russia and made ready to swallow Poland. Then, on September 1st, every available German tank was flung full-tilt against an old-fashioned Polish army whose tanks lay scattered broadcast in accordance with the conventional doctrine of cavalry and infantry support operations. And when, at the end of that hectic month, the dust had settled over the debris of their con-

quered ally in the east, the British and French had good cause to take stock in their peril and make readjustments to meet the next onslaught which seemed imminent and which, whenever it came, could be expected to be pushed home by violent massed armoured formations. But in taking stock the Allies could draw up a far from reassuring balance sheet. The French tank force remained diluted throughout every level and formation in their army (except in the DLMs) while the British had few enough tanks and many of these were absent from Europe, tied to a second, hastily improvised Armoured Division keeping watch on the Egyptian frontier from whence might come, at any moment, an Italian invasion aimed at the Suez Canal.

Between them, however, the Allies had many more tanks and several

US M2

quite as good as the best the Germans possessed. It was mainly a question of matching German organisation, method and flair. To the question of organisation the French gave immediate attention, implementing no less than four DCRs immediately the Polish campaign had demonstrated the obvious merits of the Panzer Divisions. But even this change of policy did not really represent a change of heart since there remained a solid caucus of French generals, including the Inspector-General of Tank Forces who, as 1940 came in, could argue that the lessons from Poland did not apply to France – '...in future operations the primary role of the tank will be the same as in the past: to assist the infantry in reaching successive objectives'. The DLMs (which resembled panzer divisions only in shape) were retained in their predestined cavalry role as cover to the field army, while the DCRs were

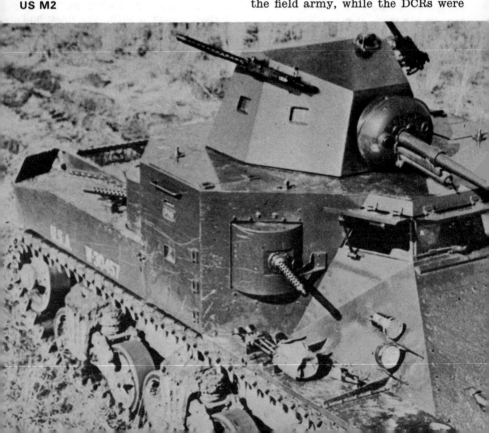

looked upon chiefly as a short range rupturing force – a role which could hardly be extended to long range pursuit for which its ponderous Char B tanks were quite unsuitable. Meanwhile no fewer than twenty-five battalions of older tanks continued to be assigned to the infantry while a number of venerable Renault FTs rusted in reserve. In Europe, in numerical terms, the French could field the following in May 1940:–
1. In the three DLMs – 582 tanks;
2. In the four DCRs – 624 tanks;
3. In the twenty-five independent battalions – 1,962 tanks. Total – 3,168 tanks plus numerous support fighting vehicles and the reserve of obsolete machines. To these could be added the following British machines:–
1. In the light armoured regiments – 210 tanks;
2. In two Infantry Tank Battalions – 100 tanks;
3. In one Armoured Division, still

located in England but almost ready for overseas – 330 tanks. Total – 640 tanks, and this gave the Allies a grand total of 3,808 tanks, plus reserves, to be set against the German operational total of 2,887 tanks of which no less than 2,060 were only light tanks to be supplemented by a reserve of a further 800 light tanks. Nor did numbers tell the whole story of Allied armoured superiority, for while the French tanks had an armour thickness up to 55mm and the British a thickness up to 60mm (indeed their new Mark II Infantry tank – the Matilda II – had armour up to 80mm thick) no German tank carried armour that was thicker than 30mm. And disparities in gun power were of a similar magnitude for only a very few German tanks carried the short, low velocity 75mm guns or 37mm high velocity guns, while the majority had only 20mm guns to be matched against an array of Allied 75s, 47s, 40s and 37s. Thus such German superiority as existed could stem only from the prowess of more efficient crews trained to take advantage of superior arrangements within the tank (and the two or three man turret layout in the German tanks gave a decided superiority over the arrangement in the French tank where one man had to command the tank as well as load the gun) and the strategic and tactical skill with which the massed panzer divisions were directed.

At dawn on 10th May 1940 the rival theories of the two leading military systems in Europe were put to the test. Meanwhile, across the Atlantic, the Americans, whose isolation and apathy were at last beginning to show signs of dissolving, but whose armoured force comprised only a single brigade of two mechanised cavalry regiments equipped with 112 light tanks, a few mechanised infantry units and a single motorised artillery regiment armed with 75mm howitzers, held their breath. If the Allies lost they might soon find themselves in the front line.

41

The nightmare

Nothing was more indicative of the bankruptcy of French military thought in 1940 than the assumption by their General Staff that, if the Germans were so rash as to indulge in mobile, offensive warfare, they would choose to repeat the theme of the old Schlieffen Plan of 1914 – the all-embracing enveloping wheel through Belgium which had been thrown back during the Battle of the Marne. Sure in their minds that, if the Germans bowed to French logic and declined to attack the Maginot Line, they would have to attack through the Low Countries – north of the tortuous, hilly and heavily wooded Ardennes – the French deployed their best motorised elements on the left flank of the Maginot Line ready to enter Belgium and stop the German drive head-on. At the same time they would send a light cavalry corps made up of mixed formations – horses and light tanks with motorised infantry – to block the Ardennes against such German light, probing forces as the French assumed could operate in the Ardennes. It is noteworthy that, in the first instance, the Germans had proposed doing precisely as the French expected by swinging massed panzer divisions through Belgium (in lieu of the old, slow moving infantry and cavalry mass of 1914). But more subtle concepts supervened and the final German plan, as put into practice on May 10th, was the very opposite of what conventional minds believed to be mandatory.

For the Germans decided to attempt nothing more than a strong feint with substantially conventional forces, supplemented by airborne and a few armoured troops, to give the impression that they were invading the Low Countries by the traditional routes to the north of the Ardennes. Then, as the bulk of the Allied mobile forces were being drawn off into Belgium, the Germans would strike with all panzer divisions united through the Ardennes, brushing aside the French cavalry screen where it barred the way to the River Meuse between Sedan and Dinant, fording the river and then debouching into the rolling plains of Northern France beyond. The essence of the German plan was secrecy, speed of implementation (implicit in all panzer operations) and sheer violence.

Allied plans to move to the assistance of the Belgians had no basis of co-operation with the latter since the Belgians had stuck strictly to the letter of neutrality and refused to take part in joint staff talks prior to the German invasion. In consequence the Allies could not be sure that Belgian defences on the River Dyle – the main line selected arbitrarily for defence by the Allies – were of any value and could only confirm their assumptions by reconnaissance after the Germans had advanced. Leading the French 1st Army Group (General Billotte) – composed of (from right to left) Second, Ninth and First French Armies – was the Cavalry Corps of General Prioux comprising the 2nd and 3rd DLMs, while on their left the fully mechanised British Expeditionary Force and the Seventh French Army completed the North East Front and extended the Allied flank to the North Sea. It was Prioux's tanks, speeding ahead of 1st Army Group, which first discovered the paucity of the Dyle defences, the initial and contagious signs of a Belgian debacle and, still more shattering, the awful upheaval created by a panzer corps at full bore. 'I was dumbfounded,' wrote Prioux, 'when I thought that the Army counted on finding a prepared position here, and would have to make a reconnaissance of the area first and then dig in. The enemy would never give them time enough for that.' It was not just a matter of time – though that was critical enough – it was a question of concentration in space, for while close on 400 tanks from the two DLMs were spreading out to cover every approach on a wide front, a similar number of German tanks in XVI Panzer Corps then in full possession of the initiative, were being thrown against a selected narrow sector opposite the vital Gembloux Gap. Thus when Prioux's tanks began to arrive along the Dyle on the evening of 10th May, after a long road march of about a hundred miles, it was

in isolation, for the Belgians were of no use and the rest of First French Army had hardly moved while its infantry tanks had to wait for nightfall on the 10th before being entrained for destinations close to the front.

The Belgian Army put up little resistance against XVI Panzer Corps and almost at once, on 12th May, Prioux's DLMs – screening the front – found themselves coming under pressure before the main armies had fully occupied their intended positions. Given freedom of movement to strike in mass, the DLMs might have shaken the Germans from the start, but a thin shield of French tanks was not only unable to resist a mass of German tanks, but was hopelessly outmanoeuvred whenever they persisted (as persist they did) in holding static positions. When forced into the open they failed in mobility and concentration for the good reason that they were not trained to that standard – orders could not be given on the move and so reaction was paralysed while the administrative system broke down from overstrain in a fast moving situation for which it was not designed. More French vehicles were swept up by the Germans from shortage of fuel than from being actually knocked out in combat, and the morale of the entire Cavalry Corps began to sag as officers and men realised that they were outclassed. Meanwhile an initial appreciation that the main German thrust was developing north of the Ardennes led the French to feed more and more of their armoured formations into that area to join the concentration of DLMs and infantry tank battalions already there. 1st DCR went to First Army to help hold the line Wavre – Namur; soon it was being reinforced by 2nd DCR and might well have been joined by 3rd DCR had not the position in the Ardennes deteriorated so much throughout 11th May and 12th when the main German thrust in the Ardennes brushed aside the light cavalry and made for the Meuse.

Mid-morning of the 13th, Prioux's DLMs came under really heavy pressure and began a phased withdrawal, bound by tactical bound, in accordance with classic covering force procedure. By late afternoon they were back on an intermediary position nine miles in advance of the main line which had yet to be fully occupied by First Army. Next morning, with a rush, XVI Panzer Corps had broken right through and were bumping into the main position which, itself, began to show signs of cracking. Caught up in the rush, those elements of the DLMs which were not overrun, could only make the best of their way to safety under the protection of the now embattled First Army – and First Army commander, General Blanchard, thinking only of holding a line, declined to concentrate them in rear as a strong mobile reserve, but distributed them amongst the infantry. 'They have . . . begun to dismember the Cavalry Corps,' complained Prioux, and indeed it was never to fight as a corps again.

At that very moment German armoured corps were making their appearance in strength on the eastern bank of the Meuse – an appearance of fatal significance, for this passage of the Ardennes by no less than seven panzer divisions had done more than rout the light cavalry divisions and poise the German mass of manoeuvre between the flanks of the Maginot Line and of the French Field Army – it exploded the theory that difficult country would be impassable to mechanised forces and flung the whole Allied system of defence into disarray. From now onwards every available French formation would have to be sent to the area Sedan – Dinant to stem the German thrust. In consequence 1st Army Group and the BEF in Belgium would be deprived of further reinforcement even had they need of it. But the pressure exerted on First French Army along the line of the Dyle by XVI Panzer Corps and other German units, when

taken in conjunction with the collapse of the Belgian Army and the penetration of the Ardennes, effected a deadly erosion of the composure of the French High Command long before combat had reached its peak of intensity at the front.

The climax on the Meuse was reached on the morning of the 13th, a few hours before the DLMs began their withdrawal to the Dyle in the north. At Sedan, Monthermé and Dinant the leading infantry of three panzer corps, heavily supported by artillery and dive-bombers, got across the river, impeded in places by strong French counter-artillery fire, but hardly ever by French tanks – and this for the good reason that the best of the French tanks were elsewhere, or had been mopped up in the 'Ardennes or, from lack of a fast reacting command system, were withheld from an immediate counter-attack. Yet a counter-attack on the German infantry before they could consolidate their first tenuous bridgehead and ferry the first of the armour to the west bank, was what the Germans most feared. In fact, they were already learning something which they had not expected: the French were not fighting with the *élan* of old and certainly with nothing like the fervour with which the Poles had fought the previous autumn.

Pressure on French Ninth Army holding the Meuse was allowed to build up because there was nothing of armoured value with which to counter-attack. The German attack at Monthermé was, indeed, temporarily contained, but by the morning of the 14th, the XIXth German Panzer Corps under the greatest exponent of German armour, General Guderian, was already beginning to break out of the bridgehead, and close by Dinant the same process got into its stride as 7th Panzer Division, under Major-General Erwin Rommel, cut loose. Faced with multiple threats to which he had no answer, the commander of Ninth Army ordered a withdrawal, on

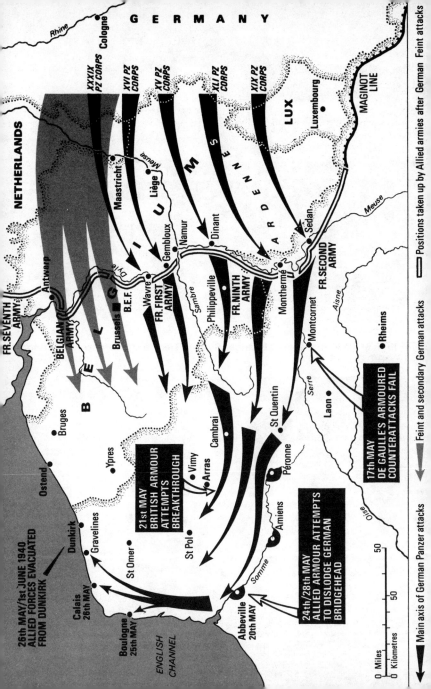

Above: French AMR on reconnaissance. *Below:* Tied to the infantry in action – the French H 35

the night of the 15th, from the Meuse – a move which completely exposed the left of Blanchard's First Army on the Dyle and compelled that General to order a step backward in conformation.

Now the whole front was in motion and pre-war concepts thrown to the winds. Now too the French refusal in pre-war days to recognise the possibilities of decision by armour recoiled upon their heads, for towards the end of the First World War it had been the Germans who had been wont to panic at the mere sight or sound of tanks and to exaggerate their numbers out of all recognition: this time the French copied the Germans of old and clogged communications with a flood of panicky messages telling of countless hordes of enemy tanks moving down every road, through every wood and field. Not only did this panic accelerate the disintegration of the army as a whole, it utterly confused the Higher Command and slowed down their reactions still further. Several judicious and, above all, quick ripostes by French armour might have saved the day – and on the evening of the 14th they still possessed the capability of making them had they known how. For while the DLMs were in course of being broken up along the line, the DCRs were still in being, 1st and 2nd under command of First Army and moving to a new stop line west of the Dyle near Philipville, 3rd DCR joining Second Army to the south of Sedan, and 4th DCR (most newly formed and short of tanks and all its infantry, but under the command of one French general – de Gaulle – who did understand the value of armour) preparing to move piecemeal to the battle zone from the south.

As the German bridgeheads shook out in pursuit of the French withdrawal, a few scattered and tentative French counter-attacks were certainly projected, but they were of no influence against the mighty German effort. On the 13th two tank battalions with infantry were ordered to attack Guderian 'immediately', but they dared not move in daylight for fear of air attack and then became so inextricably mixed up with a flood of military and civilian refugees from the front that they gave up the attempt and settled supinely into defensive positions. Yet this was by no means the last chance offered to French armour for intervention against Guderian at Sedan, for 3rd DCR, under General Brocard, was arriving with Second French Army early on the 14th and this division was presented with a golden opportunity. It arrived just as Guderian's XIX Panzer Corps turned westward and thereby exposed its flank. Thereupon, however, the miserable sickness of indecision, linked with appalling communications and a decrepit deployment drill, held back 3rd DCR from a quick, incisive thrust. There were no warning orders to the troops, no urgency, and so reconnaissance and refuelling were leisurely; moreover many Char B tanks had broken down after long marches on their tracks and were still missing. At last, with four hours of daylight left, all was ready, but then the French corps commander on the spot changed his mind and decided that he could do no more than contain the enemy – a change of heart which, when carried out, simply implied the dispersal of 3rd DCR as a string of pill-boxes along the rapidly extending southern flank of Guderian's advance – a dilution of striking power which was never remedied.

An attempt by 1st DCR, switched from First to Ninth Army, to counterattack Rommel's 7th Panzer Division on the 15th, at least got started, but then evaporated as if under a spell. The reasons were practical enough. Trucks carrying fuel were kept too far to the rear and left the Char Bs dry and isolated at the front, by-passed by the Germans who drove on without seeming to be aware of so powerful a force in their vicinity, struck occasionally by a storm of fire when they drew attention to themselves, and eventually reduced to only ten surviving tanks. The rest of 1st DCR was either knocked out or (as was the case with the majority) abandoned from shortage of fuel or the disastrous collapse of their crew's morale. Second DCR was to achieve even less since it was immediately forced to emulate the dispersal of 3rd DCR by being split up, but 4th DCR, upon arrival at Laon from the south on the 16th, at least made a gesture of aggression. This was de Gaulle's division – though hardly a division in appearance since it was improvised on the eve of battle when the general, his staff and tank units (but not the full scale of infantry and artillery), met for the first time adjacent to their first battlefield.

At least de Gaulle understood the need for haste and did not waste time waiting for the others to arrive. 'I would attack next morning with whatever forces might have reached me' – and attack he did, in a fashion, against Guderian's flank at Montcornet using a hotch–potch miscellany of tanks unsupported by infantry. But the River Serre crossed his front and helped stiffen a German defensive flank thrown out by 1st Panzer Division. Guderian, in fact, though aware that a counter-attack had taken place, dismissed it as of no importance, simply writing, 'An enemy tank company, which tried to enter the town from the south-west, was taken prisoner'. Hanging on to Guderian's coat-tails for the the next three days 4th DCR tried again and again to interfere with the Germans' progress. It was a hopeless task, for even as fresh elements were brought in to reinforce de Gaulle, the rest were being whittled away in combat on ground dominated by the enemy, and little or no assistance was forthcoming from the rest of the French Army which, almost wherever it came in contact with the Germans, dissolved in rout. On 20th May de Gaulle's division was pulled out to re-organise and refit in preparation for the next phase of

operations, for on that day the campaign reached another decisive point. The Germans had reached the Channel Coast at Abbeville and cut the Allied armies in two.

For the Allied High Command the early reverses had escalated into a nightmare of defeat with the best of their armies either cut off in Belgium or prostrate in disruption, their morale sapped to its dregs. The obvious way out of the mess – apparent to the Germans as well – would be twin converging drives from north and south to sever the head of the panzer thrust from its base and throttle those of the panzer divisions which had made their way to the coast on the 20th. On the 21st, these were busy strengthening the walls of the corridor, establishing

48

Under-gunned and ill-protected, British cavalry light tanks which suffered badly in battles with powerful German anti-tank weapons

bridgeheads over the Somme not far from Abbeville and turning north to threaten the ports of Boulogne, Calais and Dunkirk. South of the Somme, however, there was nothing of offensive value for the French to throw immediately northwards. Only from the north was anything likely to come and already plans were afoot to mount a southward driving offensive hinged on Arras. But once again the creaking, outclassed machinery of the Allied command proved unequal to the demand for speed. Instead of a great mass being hurled into the fray, only the two battalions of Matilda Marks I and II infantry tanks belonging to the British 1st Tank Brigade, along with three infantry battalions and weary remnants of the French 3rd DLM, were ready to attack on the 21st. By that time however the walls of the panzer corridor had already been lined by motorised infantry as far as Arras, and Rommel's 7th Panzer Division, which had arrived at Arras and been rebuffed by the British on the 20th, was getting ready to move off at 1400hrs in a short hook round the west of the city to plunge a new thrust into the flank of the Allied armies withdrawing slowly and irresolutely towards the coast. At that moment the slow Matildas went into action.

It was ironic that this first assault

by the Matildas should illuminate almost every misconception in the Allied use of armour. The Matildas had been designed for infantry support in deliberate attacks after careful preparation – they were not meant or designed to participate in long road marches and deep penetrations laid on in haste. Prior to the 21st, however, the Matildas had followed the BEF into Belgium, stood by inactive while the light tanks of the cavalry bore the brunt (and suffered grievous losses) in close combat of an infantry nature, been brought back to Arras on a wearing journey on their tracks of over 130 miles and were then asked to drive deep and precipitously into the German corridor – to wheel round the western outskirts of Arras on the inner reciprocal course to that being taken (all unknown) by 7th Panzer. The long road march had taken its mechanical toll and only fifty-eight Mark I and sixteen Mark II Matildas out of a hundred were present. Crews were tired and the plan they were told to carry out was crudely conceived, based on scanty information and hastily launched towards a poorly defined objective. The infantry were even wearier than the tank men and had to walk several miles from the start line on Vimy Ridge to the battle, while only one of the two field artillery batteries allocated to support the attack arrived in time to take part. Of co-ordination between tanks, infantry and guns there was precious little (and that went for co-operation with the nearby 3rd DLM as well) – of air support in a sky dominated by German aircraft there was none. It was only by miracles of improvisation that two columns of tanks, flanked by the French, set off on time – but hardly surprising that the right hand one, short of orders and innocent of maps, went astray and got partially entangled with the left hand column – and at one time came under fire from the French.

Nevertheless, these two confused tank columns, leaving their infantry further and further behind as they advanced, cut clean through 7th Panzer Division's infantry which lay exposed in the absence of the German tanks when the latter roared off ahead and got too far away to return in time to save their compatriots. The German 37mm anti-tank guns utterly failed to penetrate the thick British armour and the Matildas roamed at will, inducing the same panic amongst German infantry as

Left: The cause of the trouble – a Panzer regiment in the attack
Above: Converted to a pill box, this Char B died an immobile death

German tanks had induced amongst the French. It was only the resolute gunners of German 105mm field guns and dual purpose 88mm guns which at last acted as a longstop and brought the British to a halt – and then they only succeeded in doing so because the inadequate armament of the Matildas could not subdue the German guns when the British infantry and artillery had fallen too far behind to co-operate. With night fall the German tanks swept back to retrieve the situation and the British columns had to withdraw whence they came – and at heavy cost. Nevertheless the Germans had been stopped for the first time, and not just locally at Arras where Rommel spent several anxious hours extricating his men from the jam into which he had driven them. Then the shock of Arras reverberated throughout the entire German nervous system – in the short term halting German panzer divisions already on the coast, making some return to the assistance of Rommel. In the longer run it caused exaggerated concern for the security of the corridor and enforced a series of delaying orders upon the leading panzer divisions in their efforts to clean up Boulogne, Calais and Dunkirk.

At this moment just about the only uncommitted Allied armoured reserve – the British 1st Armoured Division – was being embarked in England, though in no great shape to indulge in conclusions with the well tried German divisions since the light tanks were hopelessly outmatched while the medium tanks, which had only just been taken over, were short of many essential parts and the crews had yet to master all their intricacies. But the war would not wait, so while a small garrison delayed the Germans at Boulogne a detachment from 1st Armoured Division, consisting of a regiment of medium and light tanks and the two motorised infantry battalions, was diverted from Cherbourg and, on the personal order of Winston Churchill, landed in Calais on 22nd May.

Calais was to be held and as much delay as possible inflicted on the German columns moving unimpeded inland, though no sooner had the tanks moved out of the port towards St Omer on the 23rd than they found themselves delayed, not only by scattered parties of Germans but also by hordes of refugees who jammed the roads in terrified confusion. At first the appearance of British tanks in the German midst caught the latter by surprise and there were several hair-raising encounters, culminating in a stand-up fight between the British tanks and 1st Panzer Division at Gravelines in which the two-pounder gun in the A13 medium tank did considerable execution amongst German light vehicles and put a complete stop to further German advances on Dunkirk by the coast road. Later attempts to strike the Germans in depth were thwarted, however, for now they were on the alert and aware that the garrison at Calais was not the sort that passively held a perimeter. The column of British tanks which next sallied out on the 24th ran into road blocks which could not be over-run or by-passed. The German net round the port was now steadily tightened and the British tanks had to revert from offensive thrusts to emergency defensive action at one threatened point after another when the infantry found themselves in difficulties. By the 26th nothing more could be achieved and the garrison was close to the point of surrender, so the few surviving tanks made a last desperate run along the beach until they reached a temporary haven within the perimeter at Dunkirk where evacuation of the BEF and French Army was already in full swing.

Allied armour in the fast contracting pocket east of Dunkirk was dying. Here and there French tanks fought back before surrender due to isolation or lack of fuel. On the southern slopes of Vimy Ridge the surviving Matildas from 1st Tank Brigade fought a brisk delaying action against 5th Panzer Division on 23rd May and again, on 27th May, raided a German bridgehead across the La Bassée canal near Givenchy. Here, as at Arras, one of Rommel's infantry battalions was caught without tank or adequate anti-tank gun support. 'The situation was very critical,' he wrote, but this time he had his own tanks close to hand and ready to drive off the British tanks. In any case the Allies had no intention of doing more than counter-attack locally. Everywhere they were in full retreat for Dunkirk and only in dire emergency did the few surviving light cavalry tanks turn to bite back. In numerous actions they had learnt bitter lessons of how vulnerable was their thin armour against enemy anti-tank guns which could penetrate them while they, armed only with machine-guns and without a cannon that would fire high-explosive shells, could but spray the enemy at extreme range. The roads of Belgium and northern France were littered with the debris of an Allied mechanised army which had failed to make use of its immense inherent power. No longer was it a case of tanks fighting to the death:

as the evacuation gained pace it was simply a matter of holding the perimeter, fending off German air and land attacks and systematically destroying as much as possible of the now inert accumulation of many years pre-war industrial production to prevent it falling into German hands.

As for the centre of battle – well, that had shifted south to the line of the Somme and, on 24th May, to the vicinity of the German bridgehead at Abbeville. What little that remained formidable of Allied armour went there with a view to attempting fresh pressure, in accordance with the ridiculously optimistic order of General Altmayer, commanding X French Corps, '. . . an advance on St Pol with the aim of relieving pressure on the BEF.' First the German bridgeheads had to be driven in between Dreuil and Picquigny as the essential prerequisite of establishing counter-bridgeheads on the opposite bank before striking northwards. But the rump of 1st British Armoured Division, which was still in the course of landing at Cherbourg when the order was given, was not in the least ready or suitable for the kind of operation which, in fact, would have been entirely appropriate to the Matilda tanks of 1st Tank Brigade had they been available. In any case the units of 2nd and 3rd Armoured Brigade were unbattleworthy, for not only had the field artillery not arrived and both infantry battalions plus a tank regiment been used up at Calais, but the five remaining regiments of tanks were without essential accessories. Guns were still in heavy preservation grease, armour-piercing shot was in short supply and màny machine-guns could not be fired because vital parts had not been issued. Moreover the actual medium cruiser tanks were the fruits of Elles' parsimony, the cheap and as yet unproven A9s and 10s with a few A13s.

Nevertheless, units of the 2nd Armoured Brigade did their best on the 24th to drive in the bridgeheads, but quite inadequate sub-units were employed in what had been regarded as only a preliminary operation. From the start 1st Armoured Division lost sight of the need for concentration and the bridgeheads remained intact. Moreover the Germans were duly warned and, since they had seized these bridgehead springboards ready for their next thrust into central France, began a quick reinforcement. Time was theirs, for Altmayer decided to wait until a really heavy force could be assembled and put in on 27th May, by which time evacuation from Dunkirk was in full swing and the need for relief redundant. The French light cavalry divisions, which had taken such a hard knock in the Ardennes, were on their way along with de Gaulle's 4th DCR – the latter forged and tempered in battle and brought partially up to strength, though leaving over thirty tanks broken down by the roadside on its 120 mile march from Laon.

The British 1st Armoured Division and the French 4th DCR attacked side by side on the 27th, but at once it became obvious that the lessons of the past fortnight had yet to be understood. The British, equipped only with fast, thinly armoured tanks, were invited to advance slowly at infantry pace, with French infantry, bound by bound against an unshaken enemy. Despite British protests that this would be fatal, the French insisted and in the absence of opposition followed the tanks with great élan to the second bound. Then the enemy came to life and though the tanks tried to fight through to the river, and suffered in consequence, the French infantry would not follow and the attack ground to a halt while the French commander considered a number of alternative plans of which the favourite was to stay on the safe, second bound and parcel the tanks out amongst the infantry in the approved and suicidal manner of many French leaders when up against a difficulty. Yet, not quite all, for de Gaulle had the

Above: Fighting a battle unsuited to their characteristics, these A 13 cruisers suffered badly at Abbeville *Below:* British Matilda Mark Is

right spirit and with his better armoured tanks stood a greater chance of breaking through to Abbeville than the faltering British on his left. Throughout the 27th and 28th he too advanced to the second bound (against scant opposition) and went on fighting as the strengthened enemy defences poured back fire in return. Tank losses mounted, and though the Germans suffered shocks in two days hard fighting, 'A profound terror of the tanks had got into the bones of our [German] soldiers . . . there was, practically speaking, nobody who had not lost beloved comrades . . .' they were yet ready to recommence the offensive and from then on there was nothing of significance to get in their way.

The final German offensive began on 5th June, conducted by panzer divisions which had recuperated from the first arduous stages of the campaign and whose confidence knew no bounds. Then, when nothing could prevent the ultimate victory, the French at last began to fight back, in places, with something like their old vigour. Shocked out of the fascination of holding continuous lines, they at last sought refuge in a sort of concentration by turning villages and copses into local fortresses and attempting to dominate the intervening open ground with fire. But fire was not enough against enemy armoured vehicles and could only be effective if driven home by mobile forces – by the very armoured forces which, in fact, had been largely dispersed and squandered in the first weeks of the campaign. German records speak of the increased fury with which their new offensive was first met, remarking upon the difficulty of prising the French out of 'hedgehogs', but once the initial penetrations had been made and the last despairing French armoured counter-attacks beaten off, there was nothing to stop the deep advance aimed at France's vitals from which no recovery could be made. Abject surrender became a mere formality.

The campaign was drawing swiftly to its close and the French fatalistically were laying down their arms. A bewildered France was no longer the place for an attenuated but angry British Army. All that remained of its armoured element was being rushed back from the Somme, engaged in a race with Rommel across the Seine to Cherbourg where ships waited to take it back to England. These survivors might be all that could stop a German invasion of Britain if and when it came.

The French mechanised force, alongside the older fashioned foot army, lay slain like a stricken monster, its entrails scattered untidily throughout the battlefield, its brain beaten in, its heart broken and torn out. Rarely before had so great an army as that fielded by the Allies in 1940 been destroyed so utterly or so quickly, and while it was true that the Germans had benefitted to the full from their greatly superior technique, it was also reasonable to have expected the French and British to put up a better show. The failure was not just a matter of poor organisation and misguided method – though these were obvious enough – but a question of contesting wills in which one side had imposed ruthless domination over that of the other. The prophecies of Fuller had been fulfilled to the letter by his German disciples. The paralysing blow had been primarily psychological and only secondarily physical; a complete nation had been pole-axed by a sudden blow from which it had been unable to recover. The eyes of the world now turned upon Britain (whose tank losses had been 700) and the questions were being asked, could she hold out long enough in a war that clearly was going to be dominated by armour, to replace the enormous material losses she had sustained and could she build a new army which could beat the Germans at their own game? It was also asked if she would even be able to hold off the Italians in the Mediterranean following their entry into the war on 10th June?

Re-birth

From the day in 1935 when Italy had unsheathed the sword and invaded Abyssinia there had been a state of political tension wherever Italian interests clashed with those of France and Britain, and this tension had worked its military influence upon the development of Allied armoured forces long before Germany went to war. The intervention of Italian tanks (alongside those of Germany) in the Spanish Civil War had been regarded with critical concern, and the sizeable Italian Armies which had always been maintained along the Franco-Italian frontier and along the Cyrenaican frontier with Egypt were thought to be serious threats. The French might easily hold their own on the mountainous Riviera, but the British Army could be in trouble in the desert since Italian rearmament had long been under way when the British had not even started.

As a minor deterrent a few British medium and light tanks, along with armoured cars and infantry, had been gathered near Mersa Matruh, hardly fit for serious combat but designed to make faces and to acquire experience of operating mechanised forces in the desert. Even so, armoured vehicles were far from new to this part of the desert. The Italians themselves had employed armoured cars in Tripolitania before the First World War and British armoured cars had fought the Senussi in Cyrenaica in 1915. Since then several adventurous pioneers, mostly British, had explored the sand seas hundreds of miles to the south of the Mediterranean coast. But it would be misleading to suggest that Europeans took willingly to life in the endless desert wastes. In fact the desert's immensity and inhospitality were quite repulsive as, in addition to the rigours imposed by primitive surroundings where it was hot by day and, in winter, cold by night, there was always the chronic fear of becoming hopelessly lost in waterless terrain.

Nevertheless, throughout the 30s, a significant number of British soldiers learnt the basic skills of desert survival and navigation – an education which assumed increased importance following each succeeding political scare. In September 1938, when the Munich crisis seemed likely to bring Britain into conflict with Italians as well as Germans, a new military step was taken: the scattered units of the Tank Corps with medium and light tanks and the recently mechanised cavalry (7th Hussars in light tanks, 8th Hussars in Ford trucks and 11th Hussars in ancient armoured cars) were at last formed into a mobile division and its command given to Hobart, rushed out at short notice from England. Hobart had to make bricks without straw, but with three years' experience of training the 1st Tank Brigade with only sparse means he at least knew where to start. 'I decided to concentrate on dispersion, flexibility, and mobility . . . to try and get the Division and formations well extended, really handy and under quick control'.

Indeed, by the time war had come in September 1939, Hobart had just about achieved his aim despite the recalcitrance of the old-fashioned machines at his disposal and the scepticism of his superiors. He was ready, but the Italians held back and Hobart ·was then denied the fruits of his labours when he was removed from command by Generals Wavell and Wilson on the grounds that they had 'no confidence in his ability to command the Armoured Division to their satisfaction', because of what they judged to be Hobart's overcentralisation of command and the heresy of his tactical ideas being based upon the invincibility of the tank to the exclusion of the employment of other arms in correct proportion. Time was to show who was right.

Immediately Italy went to war the Mobile Division, renamed the 7th Armoured Division and wearing the sign of the Jerboa (Desert Rat), raided the Italians along the frontier, sweeping in from the remoter depths of the desert where they were more at home than Italians, who clung uncomfortably to fortified posts (such as Capuzzo), because they were not nearly so well desert orientated as the British. These were the first dividends from Hobart's training and the epitome of the tactical ideas he had espoused. For the next three years the principal desert tactical move was to be this hook round the desert flank, most effective when used by the side which was best at home in the desert and therefore prepared to operate furthest from the coast.

Tactics, however, are meaningless without well trained men and adequate material to implement them – and of these none would be available to the Middle East Army (which in July 1940 was the sole British land force physically in contact with the Axis) if the British Isles were invaded and overrun by the Germans. The British Army which had returned, disorganised, from Dunkirk could muster less than 200 battleworthy tanks at the end of June and the factories were a long way short of full production. Old Medium tanks were dug out for operations alongside a mixture of light tanks, A9s, 10s, 13s and Matildas. In various stages of preparation was the next generation of tanks – Cruisers Mark V and VI (to be known respectively as Covenanter and Crusader), the Valentine and the Churchill. The new cruisers were being given a maximum armour thickness of between 40 and 50mm, the Valentine 65mm, while the Churchill would have as much as 102mm in places: speeds varied between 30mph for the cruisers and as little as 12mph with the Valentine – (all compatible with enemy tanks), but in one vital respect the British were falling behind their enemy and that was in gun power. The Germans had gone to war with the 37mm high velocity gun and the low velocity 75mm: the British had their high velocity 40mm gun which was every bit as good as the German weapons except that, unlike the 75, it could not fire a good high explosive round. After their baffling experiences against the well armoured Matildas and Char Bs, however, the Germans realised they must hasten the up-gunning of their main battle tanks, and from the summer of 1940 the 37 was steadily replaced by the short 50mm and subsequently by even more powerful versions of both the 50 and 75mm guns. The British would also have liked to replace the 40mm and in their 57mm (6-pounder gun) had a first rate weapon, but to put this gun into production in the immediate post-Dunkirk period would have meant stopping production of the 40mm at a time when any sort of gun was better than none at all. Controlled by the Prime Minister's policy that every resource must be concentrated on production, to the exclusion of research and development, the British went on churning out a mass of obsolescent weapons while cutting back on development of the next generation. In 1940 parity in

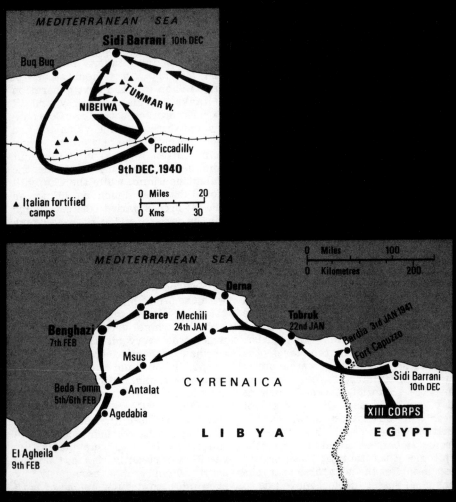

Top: O'Connor's break in – 9th December 1940. *Above:* O'Connor's pursuit –
December 1940 to February 1941

numbers and quality could have extended into a lead but for the incontrovertible need to replace the losses of Dunkirk regardless of quality. But once that lead in quality had been surrendered, the chances of regaining it got more remote with every day that passed.

Equally fundamental to the issue was the muddle into which British tank design and production drifted as the result of poor ministerial and industrial organisation bedevilled by a bifurcated tank philosophy. Just before the outbreak of war a Ministry of Supply had been formed, part of whose duties was the procurement of tanks – a task which hitherto had been the duty of the War Office. Unfortunately most of the few technically qualified officers available had to be sent to start up the new Ministry, and this bereft the War Office of nearly all its tank specialists and therefore of expert advice just when expansion was getting into full swing. At first the Ministry of Supply could only go on building those tanks already on order – that is a large number of the heavily armoured infantry tanks and a few faster, lighter cruisers in accordance with the policy which had been adopted by Elles, endorsed by the Army Council and from which there was no immediate escape. New cruisers could be ordered but it would take many months to set up production lines and train industrial labour, and this meant that for a long time there would be too many infantry tanks and too few cruisers. Meanwhile the lessons of the French reverse were being digested and showed that the invulnerability of the Matilda's armour lent credibility to infantry tanks and led to a call for new tanks with armour up to 80mm thick. But there also came an entirely reasonable demand for ten armoured divisions – five by the spring of 1941, seven by the summer and the rest by the end of that year – and armoured divisions were intended to be equipped with cruisers (which were not going to be ready) and not infantry tanks.

In the summer of 1940, in Britain, the existing 1st and 2nd Armoured Divisions were made good with new tanks straight off the production lines, while the cadres of the future divisions began to assemble and train with whatever improvisations could be devised. Although tank production was rising fast – it was 1,399 in 1940 (compared with 1,460 in Germany) and rose to 4,841 in 1941 – those numbers included a preponderance of the virtually useless light tanks and in any case fell far short of the 10,000 vehicles which the Prime Minister accepted as being necessary to fill the new armoured divisions and infantry tank units, to replace losses in battle and to create a reserve. Then demand for greater numbers increased as, once again, in Autumn 1940 and for the fourth time since 1938, the organisation of each armoured division was changed. Now it was to consist of six mixed regiments of light and medium tanks, an armoured car regiment and only one artillery but three infantry battalions – and this formation required no less than 320 tanks. If, in some instances, these could only be infantry tanks, such as the Valentine, that just had to be endured.

The provision of tanks and other essential vehicles for the armoured formations was but one important facet in the task of creating a new army with which to match the well-experienced Germans. From top to bottom the British suffered from a dire shortage of officers who really understood the problems of building, training and commanding armoured troops whose characteristics were nearly the opposite of conventional forces. Many thought they knew and tried from every level to rectify the muddle or to make do. In November Churchill was minuting for 'I' tanks in lieu of cruisers, 'We must adapt our tactics for the time to this weapon as we have no other. Meanwhile the production of cruiser tanks and of A22s must be driven forward to the

utmost limit.' But A22 was yet another heavy (soon to be known as Churchill) and therefore not suitable for the armoured divisions. In its ignorance the War Office was in no position to refute many spurious arguments, for the tank experts were in the Ministry of Supply and out of touch with the latest operational requirements and the newly set up Armoured Fighting Vehicle Directorate in the War Office was not strong enough, as yet, to make its influence felt. The recognised point of consultation between the two ministries – the Tank Board – was also weak since it had responsibility and no power and suffered from a destructive sequence of reorganisations. In the short term the Ministry of Supply could turn out existing designs, but when it came to a carefully consolidated look at the future and the casting of long term plans there could be no agreement and little progress.

Of opinions there were plenty but hardly any with authority based on experience. Most of the pre-eminent pre-war experts had been dispersed – Fuller into retirement, Broad and others to India, Pile (a member of the first Experimental Force) to the command of Anti-Aircraft Command where mobility was least in demand, and Hobart, sacked, retired and serving in the Home Guard where he did his duty as a lance-corporal. It was to Hobart that the Prime Minister now turned as the man to be put in overall charge of tanks – in effect to create what Hobart was to describe as

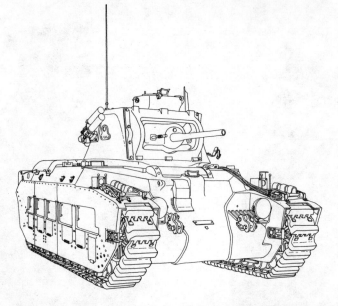

The key to the assault on the Italian desert garrisons. Matilda Mark II,
queen of the battlefield with her 80mm armour impervious to any gun.
Weight: **26 tons.** *Armament:* **1 × 40mm and 1mg.** *Speed:* **15mph.** *Range:* **70 miles**
Crew: **4**

'Wholly Armoured Battle Formations, unhampered by unarmoured formations and not tied to or clogged by Infantry formations'. This force would consist of twenty divisions including anti-aircraft, motorised artillery, infantry, engineer and parachutist units, organised by a General Officer-in-Command Armoured Army who 'must have the full support of the Army Council to carry out his task and be himself a member of the Army Council'. But this was just too much for the Army Council whose members were already somewhat shaken at the thought of Hobart in full flood out of the backwater of retirement, bubbling over in their midst. The CIGS, General Dill, temporised and offered Hobart command of one of the unformed armoured divisions or a watered down command of the Royal Armoured Corps with the task of raising and training an armoured force and then handing it over to the army for them to do with as they pleased. The speci-

fication of tank design was also specifically to be withheld from the new CRAC – above all he was not to be a member of the Army Council. To none of this could Hobart agree because he saw the pitfalls of '. . . a rotten organisation – destined to failure – and when this became apparent I should, of course, be a convenient scapegoat'. So Hobart declined and went off to form an armoured division while, in his place, they put General Martel whose promotion of tanks, since the days when he had been a member of Elles' staff in the First World War had been persistent and, from a technical point of view, more effective and dedicated than any other.

Without terms of reference, since the War Office had already found them too difficult to frame, Martel settled down to establish realistic organisations and to re-start the education of those whose job it would be to fight the armoured battles of the future. The recruitment of men was in full swing, the training organisation which was to turn them into drivers, gunners, radio operators and commanders was getting into its stride and the tactical lessons learned in France were being applied to modify existing doctrine. Senior commanders, whose minds had yet to become adjusted to the pace of armoured warfare, were being groomed or discarded and the tools of command, well trained staff officers operating their commander's wishes through specially arranged signal channels, were being gathered and taught to function with imagination and at a vastly greater speed than in the past. Partly the measure of Martel's success would be the forthcoming success of his fledgelings, as they went out to battle, and though he had no power to do more than make suggestions on the vehicles they should be given, the ensuing success or failure of British armoured forces over the next two years, at least, would be attributable to him.

Just when the British were rationalising their armour under the threat of invasion in 1940, the Americans were doing the same thing, and also in haste since the possibility of war now looked closer than it had at the beginning of the year. Late in starting, the Americans moved swiftly once the need became overwhelmingly obvious and because, as had happened before, they had studied insufficiently by themselves they were forced into the emulation of others. In July, under the inspiration of General A R Chaffee, they ruthlessly combined mechanised infantry and cavalry tank units into one United States Armored Corps based on Fort Knox – a direct copy of the German armoured arm in philosophy, since the idea of it being a decisive force in its own right was duly accepted – at last. The Experimental 7th Cavalry Brigade became the 1st Armored Brigade of the 1st Armored Division – and that division, with its equivalent of six light tank

and two medium tank battalions supported by reconnaissance, artillery and motorised units, looked remarkably like the early panzer divisions, comprising in all 700 armoured vehicles including 381 tanks. In addition, the 1st Bn 67th Infantry Regiment was to be equipped with heavy tanks, nominated as a GHQ Reserve Unit and designated as the first of many such units to work in direct support of infantry formations. Like the first panzer divisions it suffered from appalling shortages and anomalies in equipment, since, as yet, American industry was only turning out light tanks while the most advanced medium tank design was the M2A1 with only a 37mm gun and 25mm of armour. There was no settled design for a heavy tank either; moreover, not until August was a requirement for a tank with the 75mm gun defined and since this machine would take at least eighteen months to get into production, an improvisation had to be devised. This took the form of improvements to an existing experimental tank – the T5E2 – by mounting a 75mm gun in a side sponson with a limited traverse and 37mm gun with all round traverse in the turret. In due course the product of this improvisation was to be the first American medium tank to go into action, though not in American hands. But long before then armoured warfare was to escalate to new heights of violence.

The first stage in that escalation took place in the Western Desert but a few days after Martel had taken up his post as CRAC, and it came as a surprise both to the Italians (who were attacked) and the British Prime Minister in London who was unaware that an attack had been planned by General Wavell and the Desert Army. Since June, however, Wavell's Army had been forced strictly on to the defensive for only one short spell. The moral superiority gained by the 7th Armoured Division from the outset had imposed a grossly over-

Above: Light and cruiser tanks in the desert setting. *Left:* Light Mark VI tanks search for the Italian flank. *Below left:* Matildas grind forward into close combat

laden caution upon the Italian troops under Marshal Graziani and in the first three months of the war they were under constant pressure, both in the desert from the British who exacted 3,500 casualties for only 150 of their own and from Mussolini who demanded that Egypt should be invaded. At last, on September 13th, Graziani's Army emerged from its fortified encampment to advance, five divisions and 200 obsolescent tanks strong, down the coast road as far as Sidi Barrani, pecked at all the way by 7th Armoured – the light tanks and armoured cars darting in from the desert flank, supported by cruiser tanks and artillery, to pick off stragglers and create an atmosphere of uncertainty. Hopelessly outnumbered, the British could not even contemplate a stand in advance of Mersa Matruh, and in any case they wished to conserve their vehicles which were suffering a multitude of breakdowns from excessive mileage. It was rare for more than 200 of the 306 tanks to be running at one and the same time.

Then there came a long pause while the Italians dug in along a new string of fortified camps south of Sidi Barrani and began to stock up for their next forward march. That was the cue for Wavell and the commander of the Western Desert Force, Lieutenant-General Richard O'Connor (who had been Brigade Major to an early experimental brigade), to come separately but conclusively to the opinion that, since the enemy was not coming forward, he ought to be attacked. By the end of November, what was more, the means to attack were available, for the Western Desert Force had been significantly reinforced by fresh units and equipment brought out from India and the United Kingdom – the most important reinforcements being the 4th Indian Infantry Division, the 2nd Royal Tank Regiment equipped with A9, A10 and A13 cruisers and the 7th Royal Tank Regiment with the Matilda IIs, a few of which had proved almost impervious to German guns at Arras. The total cruiser force was only some seventy-five strong while there were only fifty Matildas: the remainder of the armoured element was made up from armoured cars and light tanks.

Wavell intended nothing more ambitious than a strong spoiling attack to stun the Italians in Cyrenaica before turning to crush them in Eritrea; O'Connor, though unaware of Wavell's limited aim, was prepared to take advantage of every opportunity offered by his enemy and, since he was greatly outnumbered from the start, could only rely upon surprise and the superior quality of his troops for whatever success he could hope to achieve. It was in this constant search for surprise that the genius of his generalship was to be found, but his plan, when finally evolved, owed much of its inspiration (deliberate or induced) to Fuller's Plan 1919. The widely spaced Italian camps, too far apart to be of mutual support to each other, positively invited infiltration between their minefields and anti-tank ditches by a mechanised army advancing out of the desert. Putting aside any assumption that the mere presence of an armoured force in the enemy rear close by Buq Buq would cause a collapse, O'Connor instead planned to use the 7th Armoured Division to isolate the camps from the west while 4th Indian with the Matildas broke into the camps – also from the west. In other words the medium tanks were to infiltrate the enemy rear and cause confusion while the heavy infantry tanks with marching infantry (who had been carried to the battle in lorries) were to break the front. Thereafter all could combine to pursue and destroy the enemy. This was Plan 1919 in its purest form with the added sophistication of attacking the enemy 'front' from flank and rear.

Most careful training went into the preparation of the troops for the battle. Each phase was rehearsed but the greatest secrecy was also maintained by announcing that after the first rehearsal, on 26th November, there would be a second 'rehearsal in early December – which in fact was to be the real thing. As a departure from the accepted doctrine that the infantry tanks should stay with the assaulting infantry, the Matildas were instructed to advance at their own pace, breaching the enemy defences to cause as much damage and confusion as possible and to dominate the enemy while the Indian infantry followed, as quickly as they could, to mop up what remained. The attack was timed to take place at dawn on 9th December and this meant that the slow Matildas had to be brought close to the front by 6th December in order to begin the final approach march down the exposed southern flank on the evening of 7th December along with the fast moving 7th Armoured Division. A member of 2nd RTR remembered '. . . watching the tanks ahead with their hulls hidden in drifting clouds of dust, but with each turret standing out clear and black against the fading western sky, each with two muffled heads emerging and two pennants fluttering above from the wireless aerial', and next day, '. . . a wonderful

sight, the whole desert to the north covered with a mass of dispersed vehicles – tanks, tracks and guns all moving westward with long plumes of dust rolling out behind each of them.'

It could not be hoped that the Italians would not see them, and indeed a high flying aircraft duly made its report, but the Italian Command took forty-eight hours to react and that was twenty-four hours too long. As dawn broke on the 9th, 7th Armoured Division (under the temporary command of Brigadier Caunter since the actual Commander was sick) inserted itself menacingly between the Italian frontal positions and their reserves in rear, sweeping up those few of the surprised enemy who were abroad. Meanwhile the Matildas were closing the distance to their final objectives of Nibeiwa and the Tummar Camps while the infantry debussed and moved in on foot and the artillery unlimbered and came into action with a sharp barrage directed against enemy guns and the sectors under attack. Italian tanks found outside Nibeiwa perimeter were shot to pieces, their crews caught quite unawares and in a state of undress; within the camps, as the Matildas crashed through the gaps, the infantry met next to no resistance, though the Italian gunners often went on firing until literally overrun. More than one Matilda had blood on its tracks and the Italian commander, General Maletti, was shot dead as he clambered out of his dug-out. At that the enemy collapsed in surrender. In quick succession the same medicine was administered to the other camps until, by nightfall, every objective was taken and those of the enemy who were not prisoner were flying in panic for the safety of other camps in rear.

But there was no safety in rear either, for there the 7th Armoured Division had driven right through to the coast against only slight opposition and without taking anything like the haul of prisoners gathered in

by 7th RTR and the Indians. Next day
saw the next stage of the Fuller-like
plan – the combined assault by
medium tanks and infantry with a
few Matildas brought forward to deal
with the Italian garrison at Sidi
Barrani. Here the enemy surrender
came with even greater suddenness
than before and the desert released a
seething flock of 14,000 anxious Italian
soldiery who many times out-num-
bered those desperate few British
trying to control them: the Italian
desire to resist had been utterly
extinguished by the vigour of the
British attack. And so it went on, each
successive Italian position to the east
of the Cyrenaican frontier giving up
with greater alacrity than the previous one until the problem posed to
the mechanised forces was not that of
fighting but simply of keeping their
vehicles going in sufficient numbers to
impress a beaten enemy with their
presence. For instance, on the first

**Cruiser races into action in the
North African desert**

day, no less than three Matildas
continued in action with their turrets
jammed because it seemed justifiable
'. . . to send them in because of their
moral effect.'

A pattern was now established.
With armoured cars leading, to find
gaps for tanks and motorised infantry
supported by artillery, 7th Armoured
Division would loop through the
desert and cut off each enemy pocket
in turn. If the pocket was small and
ready to organise its own capitulation
without escort, as at Buq Buq, the
armoured division would accept the
surrender and then rush off to execute
the next envelopment. But if the
place was immense and with a strong
perimeter including an anti-tank
ditch, as at Bardia, the armoured
division would merely complete the
investment and wait for an infantry

division with Matilda tanks to arrive and finish the job. General Wavell remained steadfast to his original plan to turn next on Eritrea, despite the magnitude of his success in the Western Desert, and on 11th December, while the fruits of victory had yet to be gathered, he told O'Connor to return 4th Indian Division to Egypt and continue the pursuit with 7th Armoured Division and a few small columns – with the promise that the 6th Australian Division would join him in time to storm Bardia. O'Connor was now more

In Tobruk the 7th RTR Squadron commander flies his trophy

bothered by the need to administer 20,000 prisoners than the necessity to fight, and an armoured division, being short of infantry, depended upon infantry divisions to gather its haul. Nevertheless the pursuit had crossed the frontier, mopping up pockets of Italians who had either not withdrawn into Bardia (which had been invested on 14th December) or gone right back to Tobruk whose garrison soon became aware of the 11th Hussars patrols nosing around in the desert close by. This was the very essence of mobile mechanised warfare in which petrol driven vehicles, maintained by skilled fighting mechanics, could keep up sustained pressure on a shaken

enemy so long as fuel supplies could be maintained at the front and spare parts and reserve machines dragged forward as replacements for those broken down or destroyed in combat. Here the British were practising the art quite as well as had the Germans in 1940 and were enjoying the same benefits as the Germans by finding themselves overrunning an enemy who, from the outset, had surrendered the will to fight.

Had 4th Indian Division been retained, or if there had been no delay in replacing it with 6th Australian Division, an immediate assault on Bardia might have yielded instant surrender. But the Italian artillery continued to fight on as well as ever, and though it could not hope to hold off a combined assault by all arms, it could certainly inflict prohibitive losses on the lightly armoured cruiser tanks if they tried conclusions without the backing of their own artillery – and heavy losses amongst the few remaining cruisers was the last thing O'Connor could afford if he was to maintain a viable mobile force in being to cope with a considerable body of Italian armour which, it was known, had not yet been brought to battle. Bardia had to be taken by a combined assault in which the key formation was to be 6th Australian Division, but the Australians did not arrive complete until 1st January and by then the Italians were all the better prepared to fight. Even so the perimeter was readily penetrated by the Matildas and within three days all was over and another 40,000 prisoners with 127 tanks and 462 guns had been captured.

Less than a fortnight later the same fate had overtaken Tobruk, leaving the Italians bereft of a safe haven in Cyrenaica, for the next major port, Benghazi, was over 230 miles away and practically indefensible. A total withdrawal into Tripolitania was the sole course open – and even then there was no guarantee of safety.

No sooner had Tobruk fallen than O'Connor, leaving his exhausted handful of Matildas behind, was probing westward, crossing the major track junction of Mechili on 23rd January where a strong force of enemy medium M13 tanks was brought to battle. The light tanks of the 7th Hussars were completely outclassed, but then the cruisers from 2nd RTR turned the tables and chased off the M13s whose inferior armour and 47mm gun was no match for the British 40mm gun. O'Connor very much desired to commit the entire 7th Armoured Division to pursuit followed by the Australians, but the chronic petrol shortage caused by lack of sufficient transport delayed his scheme, and it was not until 27th January that a concerted move became possible – and by then the enemy had slipped away to the north.

O'Connor always claims that what followed incurred no serious risk, for although he projected a deep thrust into the heart of country held by a numerically superior army, he felt that he could always have pulled back if he ran into trouble; at all events the fate of the nation would never be threatened. At first, Government consent for an advance to Benghazi had been withheld on the grounds that help for Greece (which had been invaded by Italy in November) and the need to conquer Italian East Africa took immediate priority, but by 31st January the embargo had been lifted and O'Connor received permission to go on – unreinforced. Only fifty cruiser and ninety-seven light tanks remained to him and these were badly in need of a refit, but when news came in of an impending Italian withdrawal from the Benghazi bulge there could be no question of waiting. On 4th February 7th Armoured Division (again commanded by Caunter) struck out across the base of the bulge making for Antelat via Msus, while the Australians fought their way along the coast road. Absolute success depended upon the armour cutting the coast road near Beda Fomm before the

Italians could drive south out of the trap.

The route across country was appalling and largely unknown. The armoured cars found tracks (many of them infested with enemy mines) and the rest of the armour followed by day and night until at mid-day on 5th February, armoured cars and some motorised infantry with artillery crossed the road just south of Beda Fomm and set up a blocking position only a few hours before the Italian Army began to arrive from the north.

The prisoners roll in

Shortly after the tanks also began to arrive at Beda Fomm itself, occupying high ground to the east of the road and making ready to take on all comers. Fighting went on into the night, lit by burning vehicles, but died away as the enemy stopped to digest this new situation and prepare a full-scale break-through. Next morning the battle was joined in earnest, and mounted in fury to a recognisable routine while over one-hundred Italian M13s backed by ample artillery tried to overcome twenty-nine cruisers and numerous light tanks. While the 11th Hussar armoured

cars and the motorised infantry blocked the road to the south and held off those of the enemy who escaped the battle near Beda Fomm, the armour hacked at each Italian attempt to throw them off the high ground overlooking the road. Manoeuvring fluently from hull-down position to hull-down position and shooting with devastating accuracy (for ammunition was short and every round had to tell) the cruisers of 2nd RTR, joined later by a few more from 1st RTR, held on while the light tanks from 3rd and 7th Hussars circled the rear of the enemy column, piled up back along the

road, and played havoc with the soft, unprotected transport in rear. At several perilous moments it seemed as if the Italians must break clear, for they fought with desperation in a struggle for survival, but always the British found that little bit extra in hand and were able to hold on because their enemy persisted in putting in a series of small attacks instead of concentrating on one mighty push in mass.

At nightfall on the 6th the situation was still in flux for though the Italians had not broken through and had suffered heavy losses, they were far from beaten, and during the night were able to slip strong columns down the road until they bumped into the 11th Hussar group. There the fighting became more desperate than ever when the position was partly overrun, but when the 25-pounder guns imposed a stop and tanks from 2nd RTR roared south from Beda Fomm to relieve the strain, the Italians broke once and for all and the battlefield suddenly blossomed with white flags. The surrounding countryside was a military graveyard on an enormous scale, for not only were over 20,000 prisoners roped in but incredible quantities of all sorts of guns and vehicles along with 101 tanks of which no less than thirty-nine were intact and most of the rest put out of action by the cruiser tanks. In return only four cruisers had been lost and the value of post-war training of their crews completely vindicated, for the British tactics of firing at the halt from hull-down positions behind a ridge, and of manoeuvring under close radio control, were vastly superior in tank - versus - tank combat to the Italian method of firing on the move and entering battle to a pre-arranged plan without the benefit of applying variations under radio control.

This was the British equivalent of the Germans' previous runaway victories: soon these two would meet again, face to face, and then it would be shown who had learnt the most.

The downward slope

The exultation which followed the victory in Cyrenaica was short lived, for even as O'Connor was framing proposals to exploit his victory by a rapid advance to Tripoli (a venture which, if carried out immediately, gave the prospect of outright conquest), Wavell was being forced still further to dilute the Desert Force (now known as XIII Corps) in order to comply with commitments to Greece and other parts of the Middle East where the Axis threat was in the ascendant. From an aggressive posture the XIII Corps was converted to one of defence. Moreover most of O'Connor's veterans were sent back to Egypt for a rest, leaving in their place a newly arrived armoured regiment (5th RTR) with no desert experience, along with the fully experienced but emasculated 6th RTR who could only be mounted in captured Italian M13 tanks, so low were British tank reserves. The Italians, on the other hand, were in the process of gaining a reinforcement of enormous potential – *Afrika Korps* – which, with other German units, was at once to dominate the Axis effort in Africa and be a deadly thorn in the British Army's side. (The story of *Afrika Korps* is to be read in Campaign Book No 1.)

On 28th February British patrols had their first brush with *Afrika Korps* and fell back. By 24th March El Agheila had fallen and the infantry and artillery of 2nd Armoured Division's Support Group were bracing themselves to hold the bottleneck at Mersa Brega while the enfeebled armour stood by in rear as a counter-attack force. On 31st March the Support Group was heavily attacked, but fought back with such determination that, momentarily, *Afrika Korps* was brought to a halt – and at that moment, had the British Divisional Commander, Major-General Gambier-Parry, launched his armour in a brisk riposte the Germans might well have been thrown back and at least deterred. *Afrika Korps* was operating within a tight margin of operational and logistical restraints and further offensive action would have had to be deferred until a vastly stronger force had been landed and brought up from Tripoli – by which time the British would also have been reinforced from Egypt. But Gambier-Parry, though an experienced member of the Royal Tank Regiment, seems not to have read the temper or pace of the armoured battle. Time there was to attack, but with darkness encroaching he held back the tanks, thus leaving Support Group in isolation. Thereafter only a total withdrawal could follow, extracting the stopper from the bottle-neck and releasing the Germans to do much as they pleased. The German tanks were in fine condition (though not fully desertworthy) while the British machines were worn out and, on average, losing one of their twenty-two cruisers and twenty-five light tanks with every ten miles run. The ex-Italian M13s were in even worse condition since their radios (improvised at the last moment) were unreliable and their fuel reserves non-existent because their engines ran on diesel while the British fuel dumps held only stocks of petrol. Tanks failed and control broke down as *Afrika Korps* stormed into the open. At one moment 5th RTR were ordered to engage enemy tanks only to discover that they were 6th RTR's M13s; at another the artillery regiment could not be found when its support was badly needed.

Counter order followed order and brewed disorder until 2nd Armoured Division disintegrated. Benghazi fell on 3rd April and a mad scramble set in towards Mechili and Tobruk, its trail littered with broken down, fuelless vehicles. O'Connor, sent up by Wavell from Egypt to restore order, could do nothing to stop the rot, and both he and Gambier-Parry, along with several more senior officers, were popped into the bag by *Afrika Korps* which, to put it mildly, could not believe its luck. Technically the German armour was no better than it had been in 1940, though it was in better running order than the British; tactically the Germans outfought the British as conclusively as the British had recently outfought the Italians. Fortunately for the British, however, even the Germans had a breaking point and that was reached when a resilient mobile defence of the Tobruk perimeter by Australian infantry and a scratch force of British tanks met Rommel just as his men reached the end of their tether. Simultaneously British mobile columns, hastily assembled from Egypt, stabilised the position on the Egyptian frontier.

Everywhere in the Middle East the situation was in flux. While the Italians collapsed in East Africa, the German advance through the Balkans had flooded into Greece and thrown the British Army into full retreat and a miniature Dunkirk. Hopelessly outnumbered, their A9 tanks had fought back momentarily but, with worn out tracks, had broken down, the subsequent withdrawal strewing a sickening trail of crippled vehicles in its wake. Workshops in Egypt were being ransacked for whatever fighting vehicles could be found, while in England, against the advice of the experts, Winston Churchill was fitting out a convoy to run the gauntlet of Axis naval and air forces through the Mediterranean with an urgently needed reinfusion of tanks and aircraft. But at best these would not be ready until June and the need to curb *Afrika Korps* in May was immediate. In a nutshell, a never-ending race had begun between the British and the Axis to build up sufficient armoured forces in the desert either to mount a pre-emptive offensive, or a raid of such strength that the other's offensive would be spoiled. The tactical emphasis focussed on the competition between tanks and guns, for in the open desert unmotorised infantry was powerless unless protected by fighting vehicles, and even when motorised had to move swiftly from one bit of tank-proof ground to another in the hope that they would not be intercepted en route. Yet neither the British nor the Axis could have sufficient tanks in 1941 to suit their purposes; the British because it took so long to ship bulky equipment, such as tanks, round the Cape to Egypt (for the Mediterranean could only be forced on desperate and rare occasions), while the Germans struggled along with the lowest priority for equipment, in view of Hitler's determination to invade Russia in June, and also had to put up with a maddening wastage when ships were sunk by the British on the short sea routes from Europe.

Both sides made the best of a bad job in the series of battles fought

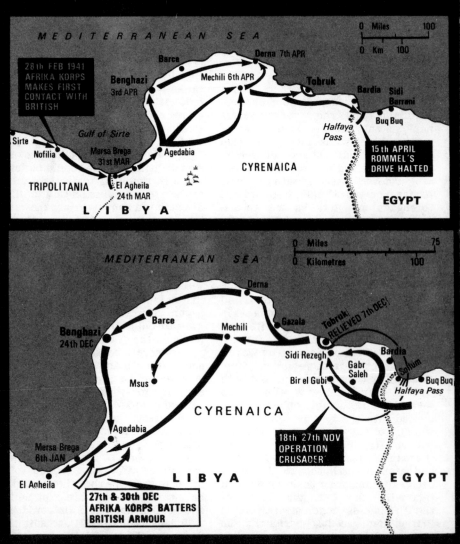

Top: Rommel's riposte to Halfaya. Above: Operation Crusader; a battle of rapidly changing fortunes

between the frontier and Tobruk. Wavell's Operation Brevity, a spoiling attack pure and simple launched on 15th May, was attempted in the hope of relieving Tobruk while Rommel's divisions were at their weakest. Unfortunately for the British Rommel was forewarned of the impending attack and though the mixed regiment of A9s and 10s from 7th Armoured Division, which delivered the customary wheel round Halfaya Pass, frightened off the local German covering force, it then took fright itself when confronted with the main body of *Afrika Korps* roaring to the rescue from the direction of Tobruk. In fact the two mobile forces missed meeting each other in the desert expanses and almost in relief, one suspects, withdrew whence they came, since neither was geared for a prolonged engagement. But at Halfaya Matilda tanks from 4th RTR scored a resounding success, breaching the enemy defences without previous announcement by an artillery bombardment and putting the Italians to flight. Here was yet another forecast of the pattern of desert war to come – the two tiered battles in which Germans and British tended to fight to the death while the Italians, all too frequently, allowed themselves to become easy meat, the weak link in any Axis defence and an attractive target for any British attack. Surprise could come, however, if the Italians should happen to fight back either of their own volition or because they were stiffened by Germans.

Without allowing the British time to consolidate Halfaya Pass, Rommel curtly threw them out on 27th May and himself put it into a much stronger state of defence, digging a few 88mm dual-purpose guns in amongst the rocks ready for the Matildas should they come that way again. And come they soon did, for Churchill's Tiger Convoy had safely made the passage to Egypt and, under pressure from the triumphant Prime Minister, Wavell could no

longer resist demands to employ the infusion of tanks at the earliest possible moment. But though Wavell could send 200 tanks into battle by 15th June to take part in Operation Battleaxe – a greatly up-scaled version of Brevity – he would by no means guarantee victory over an enemy whose strength he estimated at 300 but which was, in fact, only 170. The deficiencies inherent in Britain's lost lead in the tank race were just beginning to come to light, and were most clearly to be observed in the new Crusader cruiser with its high speed and obsolescent 40mm gun. All tanks had to be specially adapted to movement in the desert by the fitting of special filters to protect the engines from damage by heavy dust, and all Churchill's Tiger Cubs had been hastily converted on arrival in Egypt. But the Crusaders still suffered from several mechanical weaknesses due to shortage of time under development and this produced an incipient unreliability made worse by shortage of spare parts. In any case, the British crews had insufficient time in which to learn the intricacies of the Crusaders and were sent into battle in haste and a general state of unpreparedness.

The first great shock of Battleaxe was the humbling of the Matildas when they ran, unsupported by infantry or artillery, straight into the muzzles of the 88s at Halfaya. The cry of a tank squadron commander a moment before he was killed, 'They are tearing my tanks to pieces' announced a change in tactical balance. From now on the 88 would dominate and the Matilda was no longer Queen of the Battlefield; above all it had to be realised that tanks on their own against an unshaken enemy would no longer necessarily survive and therefore every enemy position which had to be assaulted could only be overcome by the combined efforts of tanks following up a bombardment by high explosive. High explosive could be delivered by aircraft (of which the British had few in 1941 and

which, in line with RAF policy, were not intended or trained to be employed in the forefront of the land battle), artillery or tanks themselves. But only a very small proportion of British tanks were armed with a gun capable of firing high explosive and so, unless the artillery could keep up with the tank advance (and in Battle-axe in the opening phase it signally failed to do so since its wheeled vehicles became bogged in soft sand) the tanks were left to the mercy of dug-in anti-tank guns. On the desert flank, west of Sollum, British tank losses rose high against dug-in guns and their numerical superiority had been worn down before Rommel's armour intervened from the north. Likewise it was British artillery which caused Rommel more trouble than British tanks, shelling him from outside tank gun range and forcing his armour to withdraw or come in too close for safety when pressing home an advantage. But *Afrika Korps* had a few Mark IV tanks with their short

75mm gun firing high explosive, and even when these did not score direct hits on British tanks they could still cripple them by knocking off vital parts (such as air cleaners), thereby raising an already high rate of break-down higher yet.

By nightfall of 15th June the British tank strength had been more than halved and when next morning the anxious armoured car crews of the 11th Hussars, guarding the north-western flank, found *Afrika Korps* sweeping round in a reciprocal desert hook, the British had to give up the offensive to save themselves. By then the balance was restored, for without their 88s the Germans possessed no advantage over the British Crusaders (when they were in working order) and the Matildas, and it was a fighting retreat by the latter which dominated *Afrika Korps'* armour on the frontier and enabled the rest of the British force to escape into Egypt without being cut off. Rommel had won another striking victory – he lost only twenty-five tanks to eight-seven British, had established a moral supremacy and, incidentally, caused the sacking of Wavell and his replacement by General Auchinleck.

Operations in the desert then paused while both sides strained to rebuild their strength, and, in any case, the desert soon took a lesser importance when the attention of the world became rivetted on the massive German invasion of Russia on 22nd June. Nevertheless, Rommel determined to take Tobruk as an essential preliminary to further operations, while the British, now consumed with the impulse of seeking tank versus tank combat, made ready an offensive whose aim, apart from the

Left: Twilight of a queen – a Matilda and crews during the Brevity, Battleaxe saga. *Below:* Kicking life into a tired A13 in Tobruk

relief of Tobruk, was the defeat of Axis armour as the tactical key to a strategic victory. Both sides meant to strike about mid-November but the British, with their Operation Crusader, were ready first. Certainly in numbers they had the edge, for on the eve of battle the Desert Army had become Eighth Army and could assemble 700 tanks including a large number of Crusaders, Valentines and Matildas and a complete brigade, over 150 tanks, of the newly arrived American Stuart light tank with its high speed, 38mm armour and out-dated 37mm gun – an obsolescent harbinger of the flood of tanks which was just beginning to pour from the American arsenals. More than ever, however, the balance of forces would be dependent upon quality, and in that respect the 200 Italian tanks of *Ariete* Armoured Division and the 120 German machines in *Afrika Korps* were quite as well crewed as the British

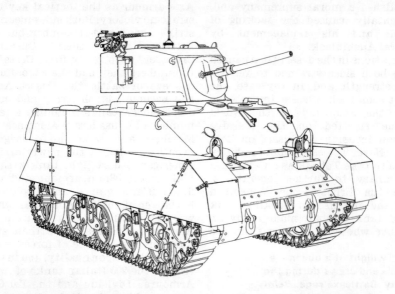

Light tank M3 (Stuart) – sometimes known as 'Honey'. The United States' first contribution to the Desert War; a 12-ton light tank developed over a decade and therefore very reliable. Yet its 37mm gun and 43mm armour put it a step behind the latest German tanks and guns. *Speed:* **35mph** *Range:* **70 miles.** *Crew:* **4**

veterans and superior to those British units which had been trained in Britain and had yet to see action for the first time. Of far greater significance was the current German up-gunning: most of their Mark III tanks now mounted the short 50mm and their infantry possessed a still more formidable gun on a field mounting – the long 50mm, to supplement the expiring 37mms and the fabulous 88s. To these the British had no counter except numbers and courage.

Once again tactics were dictated by familiar terrain and the rigorous inhibitions of desert administration. While Rommel kept his armour centrally concentrated between the frontier and Tobruk, ready to help in an attack on the fortress yet poised to fend off a British invasion over the frontier, the British planned to send their cruiser tanks in a wider sweep than that employed during Battle-axe, cutting off the Halfaya position

(which could be knocked out at leisure when the armoured battle had been won) and seeking *Afrika Korps* in battle. But since it was so much a question of 'seeking', the British had to spread their net wide and thus enter the arena in three widely separated groups whose capability to react quickly in support of each other was inferior to Rommel's ability to locate and strike each of his foes in turn. The wider British sweep was made possible, however, because they had built up vast dumps for re-supply, while Rommel remained on a tight leash because his reserves never permitted untrammelled movement.

The battle began on 18th November, though it was nearly twenty-four hours before Rommel became fully aware that he was faced with a full scale offensive and in consequence the British were almost in sight of Tobruk before there was a major encounter. From the opening shots the design of battle stood revealed, its central patterns being woven in the desert just to the south of Sidi Rezegh where the British advancing out of Egypt hoped to join hands with their garrison making a sortie from Tobruk – but where, more to the point, Rommel had positioned the major portion of his striking force. Soon British infantry had encircled the German garrisons at Halfaya and Sollum, but this was of almost trivial importance in comparison with the outcome of the mobile battle, for whoever won that would be the real victor and at liberty to snap up isolated garrisons at leisure. And it rather looked as if the British would be the losers, for their three widespread armoured brigades, backed up by motorised infantry brigades moving behind and to the flanks of the armour, were struck in succession by well co-ordinated attacks from *Afrika Korps* – and successively were written down to a shadow of their initial strength. 22nd Armoured Brigade in its first encounter on the 18th with *Ariete* lost forty out of 160 tanks; 4th Armoured Brigade, caught while dispersed on the 20th (the anniversary of the Battle of Cambrai), left behind over sixty tanks and, along with the rest of the British Armoured Force, finished up in some confusion, uncertain of where lay the enemy's main strength and short of supplies from transport columns which had lost touch in the void.

Already more sophisticated German battle tactics were beginning to tell, for though their tanks attacked brilliantly when there was an opportunity, they did so only after a screen of anti-tank guns had been pushed well forward in support. All too frequently it was upon those guns that the British were flung by leaders such as Brigadier Campbell. At Sidi Rezegh a tank driver named Jake Wardrop was witness to Campbell racing up in his car and shouting 'Follow me', '. . . and we chased after him for about half a mile round the airfield and

there they were – a long line of Mark IIIs and 50mm anti-tank guns, so we went to town on them . . . Quite frankly I was not so strong on this charging business, but we went storming in right up to these tanks, firing as we went, and then swung away a bit to go further on and beat up the artillery. I was beginning to think that we were doing fine when a shell burst just in front and the left track was broken, in fact we ran right off it.' This crew lived to fight another day, but many another, thrown haphazard into an old-fashioned charge, were not so lucky, and those who failed to return were all too often men of irreplaceable experience whose skill was wasted by bull-in-a-chinashop tactics.

The awful inadequacy of British armament was fundamental to their inferiority. They had nothing with which to match the long 50mm, the short 75 and the dual-purpose 88 – all three of which were highly effective at ranges of 1,000 yards or more. With the 40mm gun the British would be lucky to score a hit and penetrate German tanks at 800 yards and since their main armament could only fire solid shot and not HE they could only spray German guns with machine gun fire – again without much effect beyond 800 yards at the best. Only the British towed 25-pounder field gun could help restore the balance, and did so at its peril since it took time to get into and out of action, was hampered in soft sand because its tractor was only a wheeled vehicle, and could not aim such accurate anti-tank fire as a high velocity gun since its zone of dispersion, like all lower velocity guns, was high; therefore it had to fire a desperately large number of rounds to obtain the chance of a direct hit. Nevertheless this gun was the lynch pin of the British forces during Crusader and frequently was instrumental in repelling German tanks when all else had failed.

The battle came to its first crisis on 23rd November when Rommel managed to sandwich the bulk of British armour between Tobruk and Gabr Saleh as the result of his well directed turning movement to the south. Fifth South African Infantry Brigade was virtually annihilated and the armoured brigades were again taken on one by one without moving decisively to each other's assistance. On the night of the 21st/22nd a highly complex situation had arisen at Sidi Rezegh, but one thing was clear – the British XXX Corps, which contained the armoured striking force, was down to seventy tanks out of its original 500 odd. British commanders, whose optimism had been fed by gross over-estimates of the losses inflicted upon their enemy, now realised that they were on the brink of disaster – an impression that was dramatised when the Germans suddenly quitted the vital arena at Sidi Rezegh and roared off to the east in a flamboyant raid against the British rear and also as a relief force to the beleaguered garrisons at Halfaya and Sollum. Desperate as matters then seemed, with the enemy loose in the rear (so desperate to General Cunningham, the British commander, that he wanted to give up and had to be relieved of his command by General Auchinleck), this German diversion to the frontier gave a crucial respite to the British at Sidi Rezegh. For a few invaluable hours the battlefield, which was the graveyard of so many tanks, was left in British possession, giving them the opportunity to recover and repair seventy, along with other vehicles, to drive forward reinforcements and reorganise before *Afrika Korps* returned to the fray. Operation Crusader was notable, among many things, for wild fluctuations in British tank strengths – fluctuations caused by losses in action, widespread breakdowns and random replacements: on 25th November 4th Armoured Brigade could muster only forty-one tanks; on the 29th after more losses and still bigger replacements it was eighty-five,

and on the 30th had risen to 120 – and this record was copied in the other brigades.

The central battle had to return to Sidi Rezegh for so long as the British persisted in staying there; across Rommel's lines of communication, they could not be ignored. But by now a new crisis had arisen – a crisis for Rommel. He could continue to out-gun and out-fight the British, but he could not replace the losses he had incurred and went on incurring at each engagement. Moreover the British, who had been regularly reinforced

throughout the battle, now fought with greater circumspection. The commander of the sole surviving tank in a Valentine troop put it in a nutshell, 'Tanks in defence must be used on the tip and run principle in an attempt to lead the enemy onto our guns; tanks are thrown away if they are driven straight at an enemy column that has its guns well forward.'

With every day that passed Rommel's chances of prevailing declined until on 5th December, after one last unavailing lunge to save the frontier garrisons, he began to pull back towards Gazala. Yet in victory – and victory this undoubtedly was – the British had no great reason for self-congratulation. They had won mainly as the result of their vast numerical preponderance in a battle of tenacity against opponents of equal courage and determination, but it was the creative tactical ability of the Germans linked with the technical superiority of their equipment which had been a fertile sub-

A 13s advance for Battleaxe

stitute for their poverty in numbers. In the ensuing pursuit, past Gazala to Agedabia, the old lessons were hammered home whenever British armour fell foul of the reinforcements which *Afrika Korps* had at last received through Benghazi on 19th December. On 27th December, when the luckless 22nd Armoured Brigade endeavoured to outflank German armour at Agedabia, the Germans riposted with violence, temporarily surrounded the brigade and picked off thirty seven victims before pulling back with a loss of only seven of their own tanks. Again, on the 30th, the same medicine was administered though this time the score was only twenty three to seven – perhaps because the British had far fewer tanks to lose. The inevitable fall of the isolated German garrisons on the Egyptian frontier had to follow and yield its bag of 20,000 prisoners, but all in all the year ended badly for the British on a note of disquiet at their rough handling in the armoured battle. Summing up his feelings as the battle fizzled out Wardrop wrote, 'There were no Boche east of Agheila and, so far as we were concerned, they could stay there.'

It was not as if the British crews were unaware of the reasons for their inferiority. They were among the most intelligent soldiers that Britain had ever put under arms and could judge for themselves how much better equipped the Germans were. The chief reason for their dwindling confidence was the paucity of generalship. This was plain to those battle-tried men who understood the innermost secrets of mobile war and it gave pleasure when one of their company received preferment – men such as Gott, Campbell and Gatehouse winning the approbation of their juniors for deeds in the face of the enemy. It was much more dis-

Stuarts on the lookout – thin armour precluded close combat, small gun demanded it

Above: **Desert veterans: Brigadier Campbell, VC and Major-General Gott**
Left: **Crew clean the gun**

concerting to the junior officers and rank and file to see the most seasoned of their number being killed off or utterly exhausted by continual exposure to strain and to have them replaced by fresh men, such as Cunningham and his successor Ritchie, who had no real understanding of the pace and significance of mechanised war. Men such as these had imbibed the by-products of pre-war antipathy to mechanisation: a generation of leaders had been permitted to grow up many of whom were ignorant of the meaning of their age. The penalty for failures in education had to be paid in blood and morally destructive reverses. And if those set-backs were to

be repetitive at the seat of war where knowledge was gathered first hand, what chance had those in training in England to learn sufficient to fit them for battle?

In any case, no matter how important the desert battles may have seemed to the British Army and the people at home who followed its see-saw progress with bated breath, the vital struggles were taking place elsewhere – in Russia and in the Far East after Japan had entered the war on 7th December with her attack on the Americans at Pearl Harbor and the commencement of her drive into South-East Asia. These campaigns would have their repercussions on the desert battles and on the development of armour – and yet the restoration of quality in Allied armour had still to make realistic headway.

Rebuilding

Throughout 1941 the British Army could be forgiven if it became desert conscious to the exclusion of deeper thinking about the other modes of European warfare which would have to be tackled before a final decision could be reached against the Axis. The training of the new army in Britain thus became torn between the dire essentials of rebuilding a force – any force – which could repel a German invasion (and only as an eventuality go over to the offensive in an invasion of Europe) and the need to train units fit to fight in the desert. These two essentials were almost incompatible since the basic conditions of terrain were so different and training grounds which would simulate continental battlefields were hard to come by in Britain where every spare acre was required for industry or agriculture – while ground like the desert was, of course, non-existent.

When Martel took over as CRAC at the end of 1940, he had achieved great prominence for the armoured army at the right psychological moment when the general public had again been reminded by the Desert Army of the vital importance of tanks. In the allocation of the nation's best man-power, priority still went to the Royal Navy and the Royal Air Force, but the Army was also receiving a goodly proportion of the most intelligent men and sending many into the armoured forces. Martel's propaganda made a strong impression on young men and especially those who preferred to indulge in individual combat on land such as air crew undertook in the air. The training of the new armoured divisions was pushed ahead as fast as conditions would allow, but shortage of equipment and training areas, the recurrent need to milk existing units for drafts to replace losses in the Middle East and the habitual reservations of a hierarchy who still harboured doubts as to what sort of army they really wanted, held back progress when the overall need to catch up with the enemy was paramount. Nobody doubted that the British Commonwealth's real hopes of final victory could only be found in assistance from allies (of whom she had none of material worth until Russia was attacked in June 1941) after Germany's strength had been worn down by continuous combat. Numerically Britain on her own could not match the Germans; qualitatively she might do better if she put her technological house in order before it was too late, but Winston Churchill for one could not visualise beyond a vague point in the future when twenty armoured divisions could invade the continent and there find support from a mass of guerrillas rising in sympathy. It was all rather dreamlike, though in the end it would be the human raw material of those new armoured formations who would turn dreams into reality.

And these men were a mixed lot, mostly straight out of civilian life, pushed through quick courses in driving, gunnery or radio-operating in a Training Regiment and then posted to their operational unit. Of them Hobart, when starting the formation of 11th Armoured Division, wrote, 'High quality. Mostly 30–40 years of age' and 'They are the most diverse assortment . . . the Butler to Lord X standing next to a Glasgow shop assistant on one side and to a Belfast butcher on the other . . . A few of the Cavalry regimental officers seem to have the experience or imagination to realise how different they are from their peace-time recruits.'

These men deserved constructive imagination from their officers – a flood of new ideas in constant evolution to be integrated with the stream of operational knowledge flowing back from the battle fronts. There was no room for the sort of complacent confidence which prompted Martel to write '. . . I was able to settle on the organisation that we required in a comparatively short time and establish a technique for armoured warfare which had the full support of all the formation commanders. Neither the organisation nor the technique can have been very far astray for they remained unaltered throughout the War . . .' This was neither apt nor true in the act. Assuredly others permitted no such complacency as 1941 advanced.

Churchill constantly fired in questions and on 24th April minuted the Secretary of State for War and the Minister of Supply:

'I propose to hold periodical meetings to consider tank and anti-tank questions . . . I am particularly anxious that all officers attending the meeting should be encouraged to send in their suggestions as to the points which should be discussed and to express their individual views with complete freedom. I contemplate, in fact, a Tank Parliament.'

General Brooke, the Commander of Home Forces, and men such as Hobart welcomed this proposal, but to Martel it was repugnant and, 'I therefore arranged for all the armoured divisional commanders to meet me just before the meeting . . . (to agree) as to what we would say if the Prime Minister descended to these detailed matters.' In angry response Hobart would retort, 'We're a lap behind . . . we must find a short cut, new ideas, new methods, new applications. What we need more than anything else is a branch with scope and power to welcome, try out, experiment with new ideas . . . Yet when I write to urge this on Martel replies, "I think we have no time for research now."'

Tank Parliaments indubitably lost their bite under the gag applied by Martel on his fellows, but the winds of research were once more beginning to rustle, though not strongly enough to close the quality gap – indeed, for a while, that gap widened rather than narrowed. In mid 1941 permission was at last given to start production of the 57mm anti-tank gun which had lain fallow since its inception in 1938, and the first deliveries were made in September. In January 1941, following a prolonged debate, the design of a new cruiser tank to replace the Covenanter, which was demonstrably unbattleworthy, and the Crusader was put in hand with specifications that called for armour above armament with 'simplicity of operation' in third place. At the same time, however,

**British Crusaders in production –
a child of Christie's imagination**

high speed was also in demand – an almost impossible technological target without the possibility of having an engine of sufficient power and compactness available in time. Moreover, since the call for numbers remained pitched high, the chances of achieving better reliability (for which many a soldier pleaded) were also remote. It was intended that the new 57mm gun should be carried by the new cruiser, but this was only a pious hope in view of the fact that the designers could never obtain a practical directive which would enable

them to settle upon a firm design, and in any case, it still precluded the firing of as good an HE round as that of the American 75. In consequence cruiser Mark VII (called Cavalier) which appeared in prototype in 1941, was underpowered, unreliable and, to a certain extent, undergunned; that being so its production had to be deferred and re-design begun, and thus more lead time was lost and the possibility of catching up in 1942 with British models sacrificed. Indeed, by the end of 1941, it had become quite obvious that for many months, if not years, to come the British Army would have to depend upon American medium tanks (of which the Grant

character. This the Germans, who were already increasing their proportion of similar limited traverse, 'hunting tanks', were to accept and approve as they gradually lost the initiative. It was a debatable point – and far more contentious than that of armoured infantry carriers (to which the Germans were committed though never possessing sufficient) to which the British paid lip service but rarely gave high priority.

British organisation and tactics, while conditioned to a large degree by the shortcomings of equipment, were also backward. Martel was doing his best to arrive at a common doctrine through a series of study periods designed to thrash out a host of problems ranging from actual organisation to the development of command and control within those organisations, the administrative techniques required to keep them running and methods obtaining the highest degree of support from the air forces both in reconnaissance and close battlefield attack – in which, in the latter case, the RAF was still more than a little reticent to partake. By April 1941 five armoured divisions and three army tank brigades were in being in Great Britain, vying with each other for equipment, specialist manpower (particularly communicators) and training areas. There was always difficulty in making ground available, for the Army was in traditional competition with agricultural requirements at a time of food shortage, due to the U-Boat blockade, and with property owners who had feelings of dread when it looked as though they were to be visited by tracked vehicles. In the Middle East there were two armoured divisions and one army tank brigade with a third division in process of being formed from the last survivors of the old horsed cavalry, and in India the foundations of an additional three armoured and four army tank brigades were being laid. But even this was insufficient when set against Churchill's talk of an eventual

was first) to meet its cruiser demands. In these circumstances consideration had to be given to mounting the 57mm and other guns on improvised chassis without necessarily providing them with a sophisticated all-round traverse; several projects were tried out, including a 76mm gun in the hull of a Churchill, a 25-pounder field gun on a Bren gun carrier and the 57mm on a Valentine, but none found favour since the Royal Armoured Corps persisted in demanding that its armoured vehicles should be sufficiently ubiquitous to fight in *all* – especially offensive – conditions, and the self-propelled anti-tank gun was fundamentally only defensive in

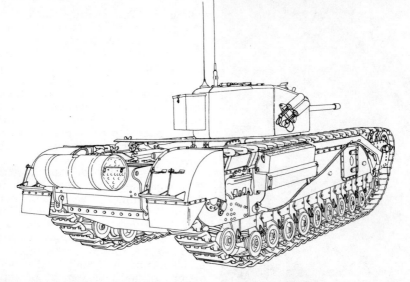

The last word in British Infantry Tanks, the Churchill suffered many mechanical vicissitudes before proving its worth in Tunisia by its toughness and agility on steep slopes. *Weight:* **39 tons.** *Armour:* **88mm.** *Armament:* **1 × 57mm and 2mgs.** *Speed:* **15mph.** *Range:* **90 miles.** *Crew:* **5**

target of twenty armoured divisions to spearhead an invasion of the Continent – and it was under his pressure that the pre-war concept of an infantry army was further eroded in order to form two more armoured divisions and a number of army tank brigades at once. As an expedient several infantry battalions were arbitrarily switched from their primary role to that of armoured warfare – a transformation which did not meet with thorough going approval from those concerned. To infantrymen the enforced acquisition of a mechanical bent as well as a sense of high mobility was even more difficult than for cavalrymen who, from upbringing, were at least imbued with an inate sense of mobility – developed as Hobart (who pursued a virulent love-hate relationship with the cavalry) would say, 'By frequent practice in nipping in and out of bed with other people's wives.'

As 1941 drew into autumn and the crops were gathered in to make more room for large scale exercises across

agricultural land, the new armoured divisions were put through their paces under the direction of Brooke, the GOC-in-C Home Forces, umpired by a certain Lieutenant-General Bernard Montgomery (of whom his brother-in-law, Hobart, wrote, 'He does not understand armour or mobility as well as he thinks he does, but he is the only Lieutenant-General ·or above whom I know who understands it at all'). Brooke, then on the eve of being appointed Chief of the Imperial General Staff, summed up his opinion of what had been achieved by a year's hard work with:

'I am delighted with the way Armoured Divisions have come on, but very disappointed at the way Higher Commanders are handling them: they have all got a great deal to learn, and the sooner they learn the better.'

These comments would soon be horribly corroborated by the handling of the armoured divisions during Operation Crusader, but since Brooke had been one of those who opposed the creation of a specialised armoured

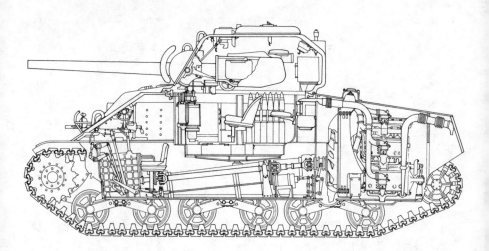

Specified in the summer of 1940, the US M4 (Sherman) first saw action in 1942 at El Alamein. One of the great tanks of the war, its 75mm gun was nevertheless outclassed by 1943; yet with variations it lasted beyond the end of the war. We*ight:* **30 tons.** *Armour:* **80mm.** *Speed:* **25mph** *Range:* **120 miles.** *Crew:* **5**

army run by the men who really understood their complexities, he was hardly in a position to complain. The Germans had long ago grouped their panzer divisions in panzer corps and were about to form panzer armies; Brooke had opposed this sort of thing, preferring to appoint armoured advisers to commanders at the higher levels of division and above – an arrangement which had been suggested immediately after the campaign in France but which, even then, was a year in finding acceptance. In the long term Brooke may have been right in his demand that each senior commander should be capable of handling armour in battle; but in the short run there was insufficient time for those who were willing (and not all were that) to learn, and in the ensuing disasters, (caused by mishandling) irreplaceable men and masses of material were being thrown away. Prudence required that conventional theories should give way to practical commonsense in the face of a problem

which could only be solved by professional experts.

Demands for specialisation in particular functions complicated matters far more for the British than the Germans. The latter had to equip and train mainly for a Continental campaign; only *Afrika Korps* had to be actually shipped to its destination and even then had no need to make amphibious assault landings. The British on the other hand, were irrevocably committed to amphibious operations to return to Europe or – later, with the Americans – to strike at the heart of the Japanese Empire. For this purpose special craft to carry special vehicles, waterproofed to enable them to wade ashore, crewed by men who understood the art of off-shore seamanship and inland combat had to be made ready – and these were consuming digressions from the relatively straight forward business of preparing to fight once they had got inland. Amongst other things amphibious specialisation ten-

ded to create soldiers who thought only of getting ashore and then staying there instead of the vital necessity of driving deep inland to strike essential strategically crippling blows. Nevertheless the intensive development and training of amphibious armoured forces that went on in Britain in 1941 was time well spent towards the day when an invasion of the hostile shore would come – but in 1941, without practical experience, only the surface of the problem could be scratched.

The scrutiny of amphibious techniques had to be even more cursory in the USA since, after the hasty inception of the Armored Force in 1940, everything had had to be concentrated on making do with what little was available, compatible with shipping as much material as could be spared to help the British. The Victory Program for all out production did not become official until 1941 and was to generate the biggest up-swing in any nation's industry that has ever been recorded, but in 1940 the USA produced only 300 tanks and of the 4,100 it turned out in 1941, the vast majority were only the light Stuarts. Nevertheless the laying down of ambitious tank production lines by General Motors, Ford and Chrysler, to name the greatest, was to swing American policy to put emphasis on quantity before quality – though in terms of reliability the American tanks of the early forties were manifestly superior to those of Britain, largely because they were founded upon basic components which had been well tested in the thirties, and which eschewed temptations to incorporate engineering sophistication where it could be done without.

The early US armoured division establishment was generously endowed in tanks and other vehicles, having a strength of 108 medium and 273 lights plus any number of tank

Making the Lees and holding them in stock with Shermans

93

Left: Training an armoured regiment – British Covenanters. *Above:* Infantry with an old medium and a new Matilda defending Britain after Dunkirk
Below: Preparing the come-back – British Churchill leaving an LCT in training

destroyers (anti-tank guns on thinly armoured chassis usually with open-topped turrets) attached for operations. It also suffered from the same sort of imbalance between tanks and infantry as the British, with twenty five tank to seven infantry companies. But at least the American infantry were better mounted for battle than their British counterparts, carried in no less than 642 half-tracked armoured carriers. Moreover, from the start, the Americans formally accepted the need to combine all arms in flexible command headquarters, creating three Combat Commands within the 1st Armored Division – each command a fully integrated and self-supporting battlegroup. But while these formations and groups were strong on paper they suffered immeasurable pangs at birth from shortage of appropriate equipment with which to train – shortages which led to subterfuge in training and the learning of false lessons. Right from the start the Americans imbibed the lessons that armour in mass, as taught by the French in 1918 and the Germans in 1940 and onward, was omnipotent. They honestly believed that a phalanx of armour, thrown fast and close locked like horsed cavalry into battle, would continue to smash its way through even the toughest anti-tank defence, reiterating the doctrine of weight and velocity *à l'outrance* without looking too closely ' at the changes which might be brought by a resurgence of the gun and armour race. In consequence they trained primarily for rapid movement in close formation at the expense of intensive combat: they practised long range strategic operations and overlooked the necessity to engage in slogging matches when movement could only be assured after fire supremacy had been achieved and battlefield obstacles, such as minefields, overcome. Like the British, however, they suffered from a dire shortage of senior commanders who had genuine insight into the nature and pace of armoured

warfare – men such as Chaffee, Patton and protégés with the temper and balanced verve of Harmon, Rose, Grow and Robinett were in desperately short supply, while the expansion of the army as a whole from a mere 458,000 (already under-officered) in 1940 to 1,795,000 in 1941 could only be at the expense of qualities of proficiency and leadership.

The Grant tank (Medium M3 in US Terminology) started to come off the production lines in July 1941 (2,000 were ready by April 1942), while its successor, the Sherman (M4) appeared in prototype in September. This latter was a major breakthrough in American tank design, for at last they had made a tank with thick armour and the good, high velocity 75mm dual purpose gun mounted in a fully rotating turret. Tactically the Sherman, like the Grant, suffered from the disadvantage of being powered by bulky radial engines which raised its silhouette and enlarged it as a target, but before the war was over nearly 50,000 Shermans were to be poured out to appear on practically every battlefield in the world. A comprehensive answer – in numbers – to any qualitative advantage possessed by its opponents.

Copying the British (from whom the Americans accepted a plethora of advice to inject into the final designs of the Grant and Sherman tanks) and other nations, the Americans also went in for heavy tanks, but stopped short almost at once at the prototype stage in face of the problem of shipping them. Most ocean-going craft and port facilities of the day could cope with lifting loads up to forty tons, but above that only specialised heavy-lift ships and a very few overseas ports (not all in the most accessible strategic places) could handle heavy tanks. Mainly for this reason, but also because of the

Highly dramatised picture of bale-out drill for US crews. In earnest it would be less formal

**British Valentine – undergunned but
reliable and tough – powered by a bus
engine and the basic vehicle for several
other fighting weapons**

desirability of keeping down combat
weight to afford economies in the size
of bridging required to carry tanks
across rivers, the Americans dropped
their heavy tank projects and concentrated on the Sherman as their
heaviest and basic main battle tank.

The Germans were by now finding
themselves at a disadvantage to the
Russians in quality of armour and
hitting power as well as numbers: in
consequence they were being forced
into a mad scramble to up-gun, up-
armour and, therefore, to increase the
size and weight of their tanks just
when the British were falling still
further behind with their future tank
designs. Thus the Western Allies
approached the tank battles of 1942
with hopes pinned on short term salvation by the Grant, a few British tanks

with improvised 57mm gun mountings and the slightly longer term expectations from the Sherman whose production, in 1942, was expected to reach 14,000. Even if they achieved a revolution in quality, the Axis could not afford to await the oncoming of this mass if they were to prevail – particularly since, in addition, Russian production was already recovering from the first disastrous cutbacks following the German invasion. As the Allied winter of dis-

content at Japanese conquests in the Far East gave way to thoughts of stabilisation and counter-offensive, the German High Command feverishly gathered all it could lay its hands on for one tremendous push into the Caucasus to wrest vital oil supplies – the life-blood of mechanised warfare – out of Russian hands and into their own. And Rommel, looking closely at British frailties, made ready to recuperate what he had lost during Crusader.

Breaking point

Right from the start of 1942 it was quite apparent that not only was the war entering its decisive phase – the phase which would determine whether or not the Axis could win before the nemesis of Allied resources overwhelmed them – but also that the nature of combat was changing fast. Germany and Japan still held the initiative and were capable of additional conquests, but they would no longer be able to conquer vastly superior numbers without paying a far heavier price than hitherto. Britain and Russia, having survived the *blitzkrieg*, knew an extra trick or two themselves and had learnt how to counteract the worst psychological effects of the bullying attack by panzer divisions and bombers.

In Russia the German panzer divisions had at last come up against an opponent with a tank – the T34/76 – which outmatched their own: to defeat it they had, perforce, to up-armour and up-gun their own tanks with the utmost expediency. As a first step they fitted the latest Mark IIIs with the long 50mm gun and the Mark IVs with a long 75 – long delayed improvements which, in due course, would make their impact on British armour in the desert. Japan's entry into the war also played an indirect part in desert battles since troops on their way to the Middle East had to be diverted instead to the Far East while 7th Armoured Brigade, resting from its exertions during Crusader, had to be hastily re-equipped· with Stuart tanks and sent post-haste to Burma. But of course the most important outcome of the Japanese intervention was the involvement of the USA in the shooting war and the dynamic effect this was bound to have on the balance of strategic and industrial power. In so far as armoured forces were concerned it mattered little that the Japanese succeeded in conquering so freely in a mainly amphibious war through the Pacific, for only light mechanised forces could ever be employed in those under-developed and maritime provinces. In Burma 7th Armoured Brigade was deprived of its power of manoeuvre on jungle tracks: the war in that part of the world would primarily be the concern of the navies and air forces. General George Marshall, the US Chief of Staff, would have to look elsewhere to employ the mass of armoured and infantry forces he had been painstakingly building. Therefore Allied strategy would have to be concentrated against the Axis in Europe, and it was to this conclusion that the Arcadia Conferences came in Washington, egged on by Marshall and Brooke and guided by Roosevelt and Churchill, at the beginning of 1942.

It was one thing, however, to decide on a strategy which aimed the main Allied effort against Germany and Italy (as well as giving first priority for assistance to Russia) but quite another to put that strategy into practice. The American industrial Victory Program (the last and really vital key to the solution of the Economic Recession of the thirties) had yet to get into its stride. Torn between the need to send vital weapons, including tanks, to the Russians and the British, the Americans starved their own army of equipment with which to train, let alone to fight. Faced with unavoidable demands from the South Pacific Theatre of operations for reinforcement, shipping to the opposite hemisphere remained temporarily in shortest supply – made worse by the depredations of the German U-Boat Campaign which came to its peak in 1942 and threatened to abrogate the Arcadia strategy before it had even taken shape.

Nevertheless the USA managed to spare a steady and significant supply of Stuart and Grant tanks for Eighth Army to join the stream of war material flowing in convoy after convoy to the Middle East via the Cape of Good Hope. But the Grants had not arrived before 21st January 1942 when the next round began in the desert war. So, unhappily for the British, they had to square up to Rommel's riposte using the same equipment in which they had been worsted before.

In much the same way as he had caught the British unprepared the previous March, Rommel hit the 1st Armoured Division, trained and newly arrived from Britain and not nearly accustomed to the desert, where it watched the exits from the defile at Mersa Brega. Struck by furious yet scientific thrusts to which it had no counter, 2nd Armoured Brigade lost nearly half its strength in less than twenty four hours – one of its units, 10th Hussars, losing no less than thirty-nine of fifty tanks on this their first outing. Yet the awful peril in which his armour now stood seemed completely to elude General Ritchie as he took his time – infantry paced time – to make deliberate arrangements to cut off Rommel's neck where it projected into the open desert. Admittedly Rommel was short of supplies (though how short Ritchie was not to know) but he boxed nimbly round the foot-fast British, who were still tyros in the art of modern warfare, and replenished his fuel stocks from what they left behind.

By 29th January Benghazi was again in German hands and the British in full retreat to the east, making for the doubtful security of a new line at Gazala, covering the approaches to Tobruk. Rommel had succeeded in spoiling British efforts to accumulate enough strength to mount another offensive, but in so doing had far outrun his own resources; now the race was on to see who first could be ready for the next confrontation. Much would depend upon deliveries of improved tanks from Germany, on the one hand, and from Britain and the USA on the other – and the emphasis would be on the word 'improved', for by the time the Axis was ready once more with 560 tanks on 26th May, the Germans had taken delivery of nineteen new more thickly armoured Mark III tanks with the long 50mm gun and there were nineteen more on the way along with a few Mark IVs with the excellent, long 75mm gun. Yet to match them the British were even better off with over a hundred 57mm portable anti-tank guns mixed in with the infantry and, out of a tank strength of 849, no less than 167 Grants. The latter promised to even scores with the much feared 88s, for at last the British tank crews would be able to stand off and shell the exposed German gunners with the dual purpose 75mm gun instead of having to close to within machine-gun range. The fact that this tank, with its high silhouette caused by the extra height needed to fit in its radial engine, had also to expose much of its bulk when aiming the limited traverse 75mm gun direct from the hull sponson, far from cancelled its other merits of reliability and good armour. In May, on paper, Eighth Army had a new menacing look.

Moreover Ritchie's plan to hold the Gazala line was also sound on paper and to be a surprise in tactical depth and technical quality to Rommel. Forced to hold a string of infantry fortified bastions (not all known or evaluated by Rommel) stretching

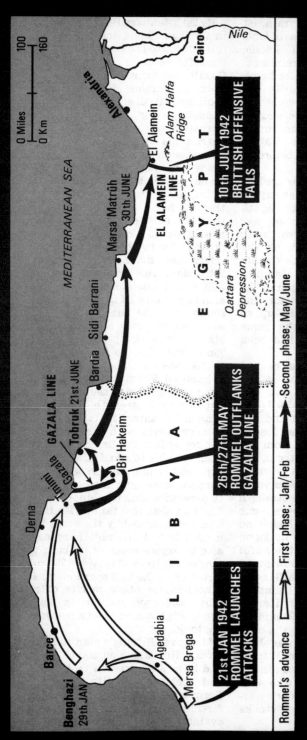

The retreat to El Alamein: a chapter of woe

south from the sea to Bir Hakeim (where a Free French infantry brigade was stationed) Ritchie retained his armour in rear of the line with its main strength, including the Grant tanks (of which Rommel had no knowledge) as part of a refused flank in the south, ready to operate anywhere along the front, but with priority as a counter should the Germans attempt an outflanking move round Bir Hakeim towards Tobruk.

This was precisely what Rommel tried on 26th May, always in the hope that the British would commit their old errors of engaging his concentrated armour piecemeal. Yet here again Ritchie, fully aware of what had gone wrong in the past, had made it plain to his corps commanders that the armour must concentrate before engaging the enemy. Thus, though General Gott's XIII Corps, with most of the infantry in the line and two Army Tank Brigades in support, was unlikely to wish to move out of its bastions to partake in a concentrated mobile battle (they had not the transport with which to do so had they wished), General Norrie's XXX Corps with two armoured divisions, which included three armoured brigades, had no excuse but to comply with Ritchie's demands. They failed to do so and failed, moreover, at once, for on the first day a motorised infantry brigade was caught unsupported and overrun while 4th Armoured Brigade, fighting in isolation, lost practically half its tanks due, in no uncertain extent, to its self-imposed commitment to battle while partially dispersed. The commander of 3rd RTR, Lieutenant-Colonel 'Pip' Roberts, described the confusion nicely when he wrote, '. . . we passed large numbers of single lorries and groups of lorries going in different directions, the resultant picture being of a somewhat disorganised musical ride . . . The brigade commander had some . . . rather discouraging news. The 5th Battalion (RTR) are practically complete – good – the 8th Hussars almost entirely incomplete – not so good – Advanced Div HQ had been "put in the bag" including the Div Commander – things must be very out of hand for that to have occurred . . .'

Out of hand they were, although next day they improved somewhat when, at last, the British armour converged upon *Afrika Korps* where it struggled to reach the coastal road. Then superior British numbers, the surprise inflicted by the Grants, and the best qualities of the soldiers asserted themselves until, with only 150 tanks left and his back to the British infantry positions and minefields, Rommel was compelled to revert to the defensive on the morning of the 29th. He had failed and in failure presented the Axis Armies in Africa to absolute destruction from one well aimed, timely blow while, momentarily, he remained fixed in place by shortage of fuel. It had to be a concerted effort, however, not a succession of solo minor attacks by infantry or tanks on their own, separated in time and space, and rarely supported by artillery. In a minor role, late on 29th May, Jake Wardrop in 5th RTR took part in a rather typical unsupported local attack, 'We shelled them from about 2,000 yards,' he wrote, 'then closed in for the kill. Maybe. it was darkness that spoiled the shooting, or these might have been extra tough kiddies, but as we closed in they bobbed up and started lacing us with 88s . . . I was closed down, but looking through the periscope I saw a greeny-white tracer of one coming straight towards us. I thought to myself, "That's ours" and there was a thump on the front . . . '

As the days passed and Rommel strove with might and main to hold on and renew the offensive, Ritchie wasted time in mounting the sort of massed counter-attack which alone could succeed. He failed to enforce large-scale co-ordination because his infantry commanders persistently gathered the armour close to them in

Above: War against Japan – their tanks did not make an important contribution. *Right;* But in Burma Stuarts had an outing

fear of being left unsupported at the mercy of Axis tanks. Theoretical considerations ruled that tanks alone seemed suitable to fight tanks – and Ritchie was mainly a theoretician because he lacked practical experience in high command. Hence dispersion increased when concentration was essential and tentative attacks on 5th June neither went in with the benefit of mass nor well arranged artillery support. British tank losses mounted with catastrophic suddenness – the immediate effects cushioned from Ritchie because the actual reserves of machines were adequate (there were 250 reserve Grants available alone) and strengths on paper concealed the breakdown in competence and confidence. The sickening smell of inadequacy stuck in British nostrils – whatever they did the Germans did better and out-smarted them – while a protracted debate of what to do next went backwards and forwards between divisional and corps commanders, Ritchie, the Army Commander, and Auchinleck at HQ Middle East Command. Theirs was a committee in session at a time when nothing less than incisive command by one man, overruling all others – right or wrong, would do. In the absence of constructive decisions the Eighth Army began to wilt, its collapse hastened when, on 11th June (after the French at Bir Hakeim had been pummelled into withdrawal after a week's siege) the Axis mobile troops debouched into the open and repeatedly brought British armour to battle on terms of Axis advantage.

British tank losses now reached almost astronomical heights – 138 lost before noon on the 13th alone and, at one awful moment, only seventy tanks fit for battle against an enemy who pressed on hard – though admittedly *Afrika Korps* itself was close to the verge of exhaustion. Numbers alone were of little account, however, when

British morale was close to the depths of despair, when an accepted calculation put only the Grant tank as the equal of the German main battle tanks, reckoning outmoded vehicles such as Valentine, Matilda, Crusader and Stuart at only one third the value of their opponents. It followed that defeated commanders, such as Ritchie, could contribute nothing more, and tired men such as General Gott (a desert warrior, from the earliest days of the war, who was losing his bite) might communicate despondency rather than hope to their dejected followers as they strove to fall back past Tobruk to the Egyptian frontier. And when Tobruk was stormed and taken in two days by 22nd June (incidentally obliterating two weak battalions of Matildas manned by 4th and 7th RTR who had shaken Rommel so seriously in May 1940 at Arras) British fortunes reached a new low. But still worse was to follow, for the horde of supplies garnered in Tobruk re-energised *Afrika Korps* for pursuit into Egypt and now the fluid battlefront shifted to Mersa Matruh where it had been when Wavell and O'Connor launched forth in December 1940.

The defences of Mersa Matruh – on paper – were even stronger than those of Gazala. Garrisoned by strong infantry formations whose holdings in 57mm guns were well maintained despite the earlier defeats, its armoured content comprised only fifty Grants and one hundred assorted older tanks armed with the 40mm gun. In theory this was a match for *Afrika Korps* with only sixty German tanks, supplemented by forty–four obsolete Italian tanks, and after its first assault had been brought to a halt in a fearful state of uncertainty among the British on 26th June, the British

had it in their power to restore completely their fortunes. But Rommel's discomforture coincided most dramatically with chronic confusion in the British camp where General Auchinleck had taken command from Ritchie on the 25th and inherited some rather vague withdrawal orders, while Gott, bordering on exhaustion and inured to defeat, made a premature assumption that his forces were again in disruption when, in fact, they were holding. At any event Gott gave the order to his armour to withdraw, when it might well have been profitable to stand. On the morning of the 27th, Rommel found the way to Egypt open and a mob of British infantry left behind for the taking.

Of all the feelings of desperation now bearing down upon the British Army those of frustrated disillusionment reinforced by fatigue were uppermost. They were well defeated by an enemy who was just as tired – if not more so – than themselves. From a position of apparent superiority they were being beaten into the ground and the armoured units which now struggled back to General Auchinleck's next line of resistance, the forty mile gap at El Alamein between the Mediterranean and the salt marsh Qattara Depression, were possibly the most despondent of all. For in their case not only the enemy regarded them as inferior – the rest of the British Army agreed, and this was rubbed in when 1st Armoured Division, feeling its way cautiously through the desert, arrived too late to take part in the first rebuff of Rommel's advance guard when it tried to break through infantry positions at Deir el Shein. But if 1st Armoured Division was ineffective it was fortunate for the British that their artillery was not and it was this arm which now con-

Left: US instructors tell the British about the Grant tank. *Above:* General Auchinleck victor at 1st Alamein

centrated a superior technique and a massive fire-power to hold back the Axis while the rest of the British Army drew breath and rebuilt its offensive capability.

The battles which raged at El Alamein throughout July were fundamentally attritional and physically controlled by artillery and infantry fighting from nodal positions. Armour – British and Axis – suddenly found itself forced to conform to this pattern since, with less room to manoeuvre than of old and driven to fighting under a torrent of artillery and air bombardment which knitted together the nearest thing to a solid front that had ever appeared in the desert, they could only indulge in a slogging match in conjunction with the other arms.

Rommel had hoped to bluster his way through to the Nile. He had failed. Having failed he could not bring

himself (even had Hitler and Mussolini so allowed) to pull back. Auchinleck's response was a series of deliberate attacks aimed at destroying the weaker Italian infantry formations as a prerequisite to loosening the hold of German armour on the narrow battlefield. Battles were fought for shallow, elongated ridges by both day and night in which the Italians would be swallowed up by combined British infantry and tank attacks backed up by artillery fire, causing *Afrika Korps* to intervene to stop the rot. The British offensive began on 10th July, almost destroying an Italian Division. German troops were rushed at once to the rescue. Two Italian Divisions were tackled on the night of 14th July and for a while the British had the key Ruweisat Ridge at their command. More than that, in fact, for the way was then clear for a breakthrough if only the British armour had been fresh and confident. The fact that it was neither and that minefields (which were increasingly clogging every battlefield and hindering mobility) hung up the tanks so that they could not follow up and catch the enemy on the run, was fatal. A characteristic riposte by *Afrika Korps* and the positions had been reversed, New Zealand infantry catching a particularly heavy blow for which they had no hesitation in blaming the

Above: Grant's crew prepares to give Rommel a shock . . . Below: But it is British infantry as well as British tanks who suffer Above right: Generals Norrie and Ritchie – the defeated

British tank units. As one said, 'there was the most intense distrust, almost hatred' of British armour.

Trying to recuperate and retain the initiative on the 22nd, Auchinleck committed to battle the fresh 23rd Armoured Brigade with its Valentine tanks straight out from Britain. They advanced behind an infantry attack which was in process of crumbling in a situation which was fluid to say the least. Lacking knowledge of the minefields and blissfully ignorant of enemy marksmanship they 'thundered past our northern flank at a great pace', a New Zealander noted, 'a real Balaclava Charge'. And so it was in outcome, for meeting and being stopped by a minefield the Valentines fell prey to German gunners who had time to pick their shots and score twenty kills without difficulty – a process which was repeated wherever this gallant brigade tried to barge through in the true spirit of sacrifice. Out of 104 tanks which went into action that morning only eleven rallied. Even so one of their diaryists could claim that the tanks performed excellently and stopped all anti-tank shells less than 88mm.

It was certainly refreshing to hear a British tank soldier give praise to his charger at a time when so many were bent on carping. Of course, the true evaluation of Allied tanks lay somewhere in between – they had virtues along with their failings and the quality of their homogeneous and cast armour plate was not to be despised. Indeed homogeneous steel could withstand far more punishment than the face hardened German plates which, though they could break up British shot at certain critical angles and ranges, was itself liable to crack when hit hard by heavy shot.

First Alamein – Auchinleck's battle which so nearly destroyed Rommel and which might have done so had he a few tank units with the fresh spirit of 23rd Brigade equipped with a new generation of tanks – marked a turning point in the desert war. While the Germans put in their last great offensive in Russia, aimed deep into the Caucasus, a new style of armoured warfare was about to commence in Egypt under new British leaders – Generals Alexander and Montgomery – who brought fresh ideas to a sterile situation.

Riposte - the taking of Africa

Montgomery was clear on two things in particular when he arrived in the desert. First that Eighth Army was badly in need of training as part of a process of rehabilitation and, second, that it would have to fight another defensive action before it could go over to the offensive. In strengthening the defences of Alamein throughout August he established a strong lay-back position along the Alam Halfa Ridge where he hoped to lure the Axis to destruction against the anti-tank guns of his armour and field artillery. The taking of Alam Halfa Ridge would be an essential preliminary to any subsequent advance Rommel might make towards Alexandria, and Montgomery's men were told to fight strictly with self-preservation in mind, from concealed positions, only exposing themselves to fire when the enemy were squarely in their sights; specifically there was to be no rushing headlong against the enemy should local successes be won.

Thus when Rommel wheeled his armour south, along the edge of the Qattara Depression on 30th August, and then north to seize the Alam Halfa Ridge, he played into Montgomery's hands and in the initial fighting on the approaches to the ridge the only surprise enjoyed by Rommel was the

technical one in the employment of the newest Mark IV tanks with their long 75mm guns. 'Pip' Robert's 22nd Armoured Brigade, on the ridge, found itself the target for the main German effort and quickly spotted the new Mark IVs, not only because of the conspicuous long gun but also from the fact that they were leading the assault and not lying back in support as had been the tactic of the older models. 'I warn all units over the air not to fire until the enemy are within 1,000 yards; . . . and then in a few seconds the County of London Yeomanry open fire. Once one is in the middle of a battle time is difficult to judge, but it seems only a few minutes before nearly all the tanks of the Grant squadron of the CLY are on fire. The new German 75mm gun is taking a heavy toll.'

This was the crux of the matter. Despite fighting from positions of disadvantage these few up-gunned Mark IVs caused damage out of all proportion to their numbers and a crisis was averted by the British because they were so strong in numbers, well positioned and carefully led. No longer could Rommel rely upon his old enemies sacrificing themselves in a worthless charge. The pattern of armoured battles – and therefore warfare as a whole because armour still called the tune – was in revolution.

In Russia throughout the summer of 1942 the Germans hurled themselves towards the Caucasus oilfields which were vital to their future participation in mechanised war, but they also diverted an ever increasing proportion of their strength against Stalingrad and thus weakened the drive for oil. Nevertheless, in Washington and London it was realised that the future of the war revolved around help for the Russians and giving succour for the Middle East; the grand strategic debate on short term plans was governed by this, but with a longer view there came the Allies' decision to invade French North West Africa as part of a vast design to clear the African shores from end to end and reopen the Mediterranean to Allied shipping. This, to General Marshall and some of his colleagues, had been of secondary importance compared with the need to invade Europe as a more direct means of bringing pressure to bear on the Axis and aid to the hard-pressed Russians. But the North African strategy was compulsive not only because the Allies could not raise sufficiently strong forces to throw a viable force ashore in Europe, but also because the threat to Middle East oil with Rommel approaching the Suez Canal could not be ignored. When Tobruk fell Roosevelt had immediately withdrawn the first of the new Sherman tanks which had been issued to 1st US Armored Division in order to send them as an urgent reinforcement to the British in Egypt – a goodwill offering which was to receive much prominence as such but which, in fact, was the lesser of two evils when the alternative was to send 1st Armored Division itself – a move that was logistically forbidding.

This was the first infusion of Shermans the British were to receive in a year when their armoured formations, hammered by battle, at last took more progressive than regressive steps. Tanks with the 57mm gun were coming into action – the Crusader Mark III in the Middle East and the Churchill Mark III in Great Britain. And though the destruction of the Canadian manned Churchill squadron which struggled ashore in the raid at Dieppe on 19th August was hardly an auspicious introduction, it at least went to demonstrate the invulnerability of this tank's thick armour to all but the biggest German guns. Earlier in the year the organisation of the armoured divisions was altered by the substitution of a lorry-borne infantry brigade for one of the two armoured brigades, merely a copy of what the Germans had already done before the invasion of Russia, but it reflected an increasing awareness of the necessity for closer collaboration between tanks and infantry if the rising power of anti-tank guns, when they covered fortified positions along with minefields, were to be overcome. Of his first experience with the new organisation during an exercise in the spring of 1942 Hobart wrote: 'Of course I think the organisation half-boiled and in fact all wrong. But in the actual jobs we had (we never had to meet another armoured div and the country is the closest and most unsuitable for mobile tank work that you could find) it worked all right.' This was fair comment and pointed to the need for flexible formations which could be employed over the widest variety of terrain or for a need of special formations in peculiar country. Certainly the balanced formation with infantry and armoured units in equal proportion seemed a better proposition than yet another experimental British formation, the so-called Mixed Division, in which two infantry brigades were established permanently with a single infantry tank brigade. The Americans had yet to try out their tank-heavy armoured division and their infantry divisions with associated tank battalions, but that moment would come when the Allies landed, side by side, in North West

Lieutenant-General Montgomery. His Alam Halfa victory marked the turning point in the desert war

Africa since each type of new formation was allocated to that task.

In the meantime the technical intelligence staffs waited tensely for the appearance of the next generation of Axis tanks and guns – realising that the up-gunned Mark IIIs and IVs already disclosed could only be stop-gap measures. In September 1942 the German Tiger appeared on the Leningrad front, the first reports of its extremely thick armour and 88mm gun a portent of a terrible threat, for Tiger could not be penetrated frontally by a single Allied anti-tank gun then in service and yet could easily hole any Allied tank at ranges below 1,200 yards – and often at ranges up to 2,000 yards. This discovery practically coincided with certain basic Allied decisions on the future of their own armoured fighting vehicles.

In May 1942 the Americans began to design a successor to Sherman – the T20 – which was to make use of parts from the Sherman but which would be better armoured and armed with the more powerful 76mm gun. In Britain the failure of Cavalier led to a plethora of attempts at redemption including no less than four abandoned and time consuming 'paper' studies, but at last a project numbered A27M was accepted and later became known as Cromwell. This twenty-seven-ton

cruiser, with armour 76mm thick, was first armed with the 57mm gun but later given a British version of the American 75mm which matched that mounted on Sherman. Design work carried on in late 1942 could not be expected to produce a successor to Crusader before late 1943 and by then even the 75mm gun would be out-classed if the Germans continued their current rate of improvement. But since the latest British anti-tank gun – the 76.2mm or 17-pounder – had progressed well towards production, the soldiers naturally demanded that it should be mounted in a tank. At once, however, the same resistance as had once held back the adoption of the 57mm was thrown in the way of this weapon. A suggestion that the 76.2mm should be mounted in the Sherman was turned down by the Ministry of Supply as impractical. Instead they dallied with mounting the gun in Challenger – an unsatisfactory and clumsy version of Cromwell – and in so doing brought to light the improvidence of Cromwell's initial design: its chassis was too small to take a turret of sufficiently large diameter to contain the length of recoil from such a big gun. So if Sherman was impractical the British could not have a 76.2mm gun in any tank until they had produced a completely original design tailor-made for the gun – and that might not be until late in 1944 and disastrously late.

A less tactically battleworthy way out of this dilemma was to copy the Germans and Russians who, when in possession of a new gun that was too big and powerful to be mounted in the all-round traversing turret of any existing tank, did without all-round traverse and mounted the gun in a hull with only limited traverse. These self-propelled guns were used either to back up armoured divisions or to give close support to infantry – and as the Germans reverted steadily to the defensive the employment of such basically defensive vehicles became acceptable. But a full blown tank was always a better proposition in offensive operations and neither Germans, Russians, British nor Americans ever lost sight for long of the fact that tanks *were* offensive and that even defensive tactics depended on offensive postures. Hence the British were far from entirely wrong to relegate self-propelled guns to low priority if they could churn out and crew a number of tanks which, even though inferior, could operate with a chance of survival close to infantry. Nevertheless the self-propelled anti-tank gun found some favour with the Allies, though more with the Americans than the British. The US M10 with its 76mm gun led the way and was to be the chassis for other guns of even heavier calibre, but while the British hull-mounted 76mm guns in a few Churchills, they gave far greater priority to putting 57mms in the turrets of Crusaders and Valentines and to pressing ahead with a scheme to mount the 76.2mm in a backward facing, limited traverse mounting on the Valentine.

Along with the more obvious attempts at up-gunning and thickening of armour went a perpetual search for ways of improving the performance of those guns already in service by giving them better ammunition. It had been found that the ordinary solid shot fired by the 40 and 57mm guns shattered on face-hardened German armour at certain critical ranges. To prevent 'shatter' a cap was placed on the ordinary shot making Armour Piercing Capped Shot (APC). Later, in an effort to increase velocity by improved streamlining, a so-called Ballistic Cap was added making Armour Piercing Capped Ballistic Capped Shot (APCBC). APC was ready for the 57mm guns by October 1942 and APCBC soon after, though not in quantity for the battles which were about to commence in North Africa. On the other hand, the discovery in 1942 of the Germans' use of face-hardened armour could be exploited immediately with 76.2mm shot so that

its capped ammunition could come into service along with the gun. Strangely enough, however, even though the enormous advantage of the 75mm high explosive round had been amply demonstrated in battle, there was no great drive behind the immediate production of a similar round for the 76.2 – and perhaps this was because the British General Staff were so absorbed at the critical moment of 76.2mm's design and production with settling large-scale production of the 57mm weapon. Intent on the short-term they failed to envisage the future with zeal and imagination.

The quality of Allied armour plate was nearly always high. Quantity production and selection of the right sort was more often the problem, but once the Americans had built bigger foundries which could mass produce large castings they concentrated on casting as many turrets and hull sections as possible and by so doing, reduced the need to 'joint' plates with the commensurate difficulty in production. The British tended more to the use of jointed, homogeneous plate because their industry was already orientated that way and there was no time for vast capital plant reorganisation: for this reason, largely, they only turned over slowly from rivetting and bolting joints to welding them. And in their case a special problem arose over supplies of nickel – an important ingredient of armour plate itself, because the aircraft industry received higher priority than tanks for this metal and so the nickel content in tank armour had to be reduced – a challenge which was accepted and overcome by the metallurgists mainly by the institution of strict quality control, though also with an increase in cost.

At any rate, it was with 37, 40, 57 and 75mm guns in Stuarts, Valentines, Crusaders, Grants and Shermans (over a thousand all told) that the British pitted themselves against a total of 489 German Mark IIIs and IVs

Clearing the African shores

and Italian M13s at El Alamein on 23rd October. And to back them was a strong assembly of 57mm anti-tank guns with the infantry and a few 25-pounder self-propelled guns carried in the new American built, tracked Sexton. But if this army was at last beginning to look like the tracked ideal of Fuller's imagination, the battle it fought was unlike anything Fuller had dreamed of in 1919. For Montgomery now put a policy into practice of which his predecessors had spoken but rarely implemented. Reversing the old concept, he aimed to destroy his enemy's infantry formations before tackling their armour. As part and parcel of this policy he planned to make XXX Corps (stronger in infantry than armoured formations) blast a hole in the Axis position, where it was dug in behind thick minefields, and then force the strong, armoured X Corps on to 'ground of its own choosing *astride the enemy supply routes;* the enemy armour would deploy against it, and be destroyed, probably piecemeal, as I hoped to keep it dispersed as long as possible.' To enforce that dispersal he arranged for XIII Corps (with one armoured division) to carry out a series of diversionary attacks to the south of the line, away from the main attack in the north.

Had Montgomery been fully aware of the widespread dispersion already adopted by the Axis armour and that concentration followed by commitment to mobile operations was almost the last thing that it would risk in view of a fuel famine, he would have been even more sanguine than already. His plan, although suffering variations in detail, was largely carried out to order – the British artillery and air forces soaked the battlefield and rearward areas in high explosive, infantry helped by closely supporting tanks followed up while engineers (marginally assisted by a handful of special 'flail' mine sweeping tanks) toiled perilously to clear gaps to let vehicles through and eventually the

mass of armour and anti-tank guns broke into the heart of the Axis position there to grapple with repetitive – and piecemeal – attacks by fragmentary bodies of Axis armour. Violently the armour of both sides began to wear each other down at about the same rate as the infantry were doing the same to each other. Losses such as these were highly repugnant to many British tank leaders of the old school, but their protests to Montgomery almost invariably received the same answer – 'the armour must and would get forward'. With an absolute superiority in resources this was entirely justifiable but it would have been less so had not Montgomery been prepared to adjust the direction of each attritional thrust in search of those fresh Axis weaknesses which had been induced by preceding operations. Losses of twenty-five Valentines out of forty-four by 50th RTR working with 51st Highland Division on October 23rd/24th and of eighty-seven tanks by 9th Armoured Brigade (75 per cent of its strength) on 2nd November were justifiable providing the Axis lost tanks at the same rate and that, when the break came, there was a pursuit force, fresh and ready with a clear directive and ample fuel to dash after the retreating enemy and scoop him up in entirety. Throughout the battle Montgomery carried out a series of regroupings of his armour ready for the supreme moment of the breakout, but when it came on 3rd November the arrangements for exploitation fell down.

In narrow minefield gaps and choking dust X Corps became involved with the emaciated remnants of *Afrika Korps* just as the latter began a tentative withdrawal. Wheeling too closely, the British Corps missed its target, became entangled in the minefields and thus created a traffic block in the way of the main pursuit force (the New Zealand Division with 4th and 9th Armoured Brigades) which was meant to strike well to the south and head a much more ambitious sweep round the desert flank to the coast at Fuka. The delays were fatal and the main Axis mobile force – what little remained – had escaped before the movement was complete. When at last the pursuit restarted and headed off westward on 5th November it was to run out of fuel in sticky going, caused by heavy rain, because too much ammunition and not enough fuel had been loaded into the lorries.

Yet this was the pattern of many a Montgomery offensive and as such it dulled the gleam of his successes – nearly always professional and salutary as they were but only rarely all embracing. It was a pattern, however, to which British armour was to conform – indeed had to conform in the face of changing values – for many a battle, over long stages of hundreds of miles to the frontiers of Tunisia, across the littered battlefields of the earlier campaigns, past the old high water mark at Mersa Brega and through Tripoli to Medenine by 17th February, without a single set-back.

By then the entire aspect of the war had changed. The Germans had been stopped in the Caucasus and annihilated at Stalingrad, and with these comprehensive defeats the prospects of their acquiring an abundance of oil had vanished for ever. Moreover the strength and élan of the panzer divisions had fallen to a low ebb – though not so low that they lacked a central reserve or immense powers of recuperation.

None of these things were apparent at the time of Alamein or when the Allied Armada set sail from the United States and Britain to land troops at Casablanca, Oran and Algiers. At that moment, to Allied intelligence, the Axis looked as forbiddingly strong as ever both on land, sea and air, and even though the initial landings were expected only to be opposed by French forces (if opposed they were to be at all) an easy victory was not to be taken for granted if once the Axis

decided to reinforce Tunisia from Europe and join those forces to the defeated Rommel retiring out of Egypt and Cyrenaica.

Operation Torch was the first great Allied amphibious operation of the war and its launching against the beaches of North Africa was to be as formative of future Allied landing techniques as Montgomery's tactics at Alamein were formative of the British way in armoured warfare. The bulk of the troops who led the seaborne assault had need, largely for the political reason of mollifying the French, to be American and the main element was infantry for the very good reason that a tank which could swim in the van of an assault was not yet in service and hardly any tank landing craft were available. It was hoped that the French would not resist, though if they did they were not expected to achieve much since their equipment – above all their tanks – were hopelessly out of date, the tattered left-overs from the army which had been humiliated in 1940. Only a few DIs, Somuas and light tanks – some the Renaults of First World War origin – could be scraped together, and none were at the water's edge when the first American armour came ashore at dawn on 8th November 1942. But everywhere the French were ready to resist – though with widely differing degrees of enthusiasm.

At Safi, 140 miles to the west of Casablanca, the infantry got as far as the shore and then, pinned by fire, waited for tanks to arrive and unpin them. But the tanks had been in ships' holds during a long sea voyage from the USA and (first lesson of the battle) had not received sufficient maintenance during the voyage. Then those which did not break down landed in deep surf and were swamped – and not until they had been dried out were the infantry prepared to advance, though they did so with alacrity once a few tanks started up. That was the second hard lesson learnt by the men of 2nd US Armored Division (under

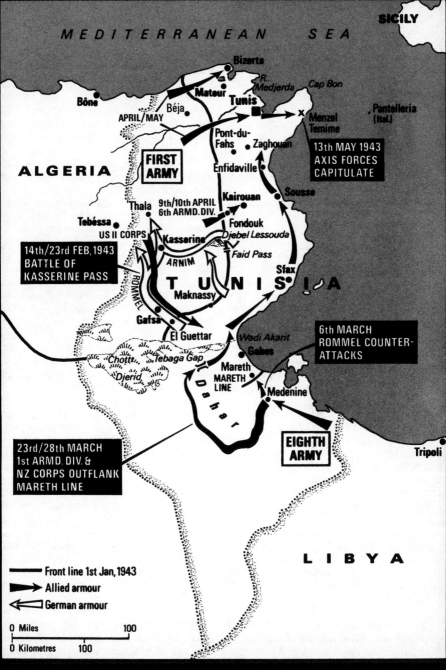

SICILY

MEDITERRANEAN SEA

Bône

Bizerta

Mateur

R. Medjerda

Cap Bon

Pantelleria (Ital.)

Béja

Tunis

× Menzel Temime

ALGERIA

APRIL/MAY

FIRST ARMY

Pont-du-Fahs

Zaghouan

**13th MAY 1943
AXIS FORCES
CAPITULATE**

Enfidaville

Thala

9th/10th APRIL
6th ARMD. DIV.

Kairouan

Sousse

Tebéssa

US II CORPS

Fondouk

Djebel Lessouda

**14th/23rd FEB, 1943
BATTLE OF
KASSERINE PASS**

Kasserine

ARNIM

Faid Pass

Sfax

T U N I S I A

ROMMEL

Maknassy

Gafsa

El Guettar

Wadi Akarit

Gabes

**6th MARCH
ROMMEL COUNTER-
ATTACKS**

Chott Djerid

Tebaga Gap

Mareth
**MARETH
LINE**

Medenine

Dahar

**23rd/28th MARCH
1st ARMD. DIV. &
NZ CORPS OUTFLANK
MARETH LINE**

**EIGHTH
ARMY**

Tripoli

L I B Y A

——— Front line 1st Jan, 1943
►►► Allied armour
◄◄◄ German armour

0 Miles   100
0 Kilometres   100

Tunisia ; Thrust and counter thrust

their aggressive commander Ernest Harmon) in this their first action. On the other side of Casablanca, close by Port Lyauty, the third major lesson was learned – that of the need to prepare for action with the greatest attention to detail. Here, when a sharp French tank counter-attack came in, it was defeated much more by the sheer volume of fire from American tanks than its accuracy, for the telescopic gun sights had not been properly aligned to the muzzle axis with the result that shooting was wildly inaccurate to say the least.

The fourth lesson – a false one as the British could have told them – was learnt by the men of CCB of 1st Armored Division at Oran two days after the landing. Brought to the outskirts of the beleaguered city by magnificent dash and verve, the last tactical bound was covered at the charge – a phalanx of tanks, armoured infantry and guns pouring cross country against scattered and half-hearted artillery fire to enter the city in triumph. This sort of movement was what the division had been told would work and it had, but against an insignificant opponent.

By 11th November Allied forces had a firm grip on the ports of Casablanca, Oran and Algiers, the French were negotiating a new alliance, and already the First British Army, brought in on the heels of the Americans, was racing eastward by sea and land to fasten a grip, if they could, on Tunisia. Until the ports of Bizerta and Tunis were in their hands the campaign was not won. This the Germans understood equally well and it was through those same ports that reinforcements were already beginning to arrive while Rommel pulled back on the first phase of his retreat from Alamein. The armoured element of First Army (which, in fact, for the whole of the critical race to Tunis added up to little more than an infantry division) was Blade Force – an Armoured Regimental Group formed round 17th/21st Lancers

to which various other British and American units were attached as the battle progressed and occasion demanded. Equipped with Valentines with 40mm and Crusaders with 57mm guns it had as much hope of defeating the latest German tanks as had Eighth Army the previous June – and it was not to know that the elements of 90th German Corps crossing the Sicilian Straits included not only the latest versions of Mark III and IV tanks but also four Tigers – the advance party of a whole battalion waiting shipment.

By dint of sheer perseverance Blade Force got to within just a few miles of Tunis, fending off the first light panzer attacks from the flank, and when joined by the Stuart tanks of 1st Armored Regiment on 25th November, enacting a daring raid when the American tanks infiltrated deep into the enemy lines and shot up Djedeida airfield for a score of twenty dive-bombers destroyed on the ground against the loss of only one tank. Had Colonel Hull – in command of Blade Force – a few more tanks and, in his opinion, more infantry to spare, he might have been in Tunis that night. Assuredly General Nehring, the Axis leader, was brought to the blackest of conclusions, his resolve stiffened only by a rebuke from his C-in-C, Field-Marshal Kesselring, and the order to rebound on the offensive.

Kesselring was right. His forces had won the battle of the build-up and at that moment were numerically and qualitatively superior to the Allies. A quick two-handed punch by 10th Panzer Division had the Anglo-Americans reeling out of the plains into the mountains where infantry took precedence over tanks. But in the plains, on the way back, the German panzers showed complete mastery over the unfledged Allies in the art of warfare. Seeming to have heard nothing of the fallacy of charging an unshaken enemy, both British and Americans repeatedly dashed headlong against anti-tank

Above: Dieppe; Churchills which never left the shore. *Below:* And one which did

guns in position or ran carelessly into ambushes laid by enemy tanks from concealed positions, as this extract from 17th/21st Lancer's history shows:

'The Regiment (less C Squadron) had a total strength (on 1st December) of seventeen Valentines and seven Crusaders, and was doing much needed maintenance when news came that the Germans were attacking. They had formed up in their traditional manner with tanks and half-tracks full of infantry, opened a heavy artillery barrage and a dive-bomber attack and moved forward . . . B Squadron and RHQ advanced to meet the attack, but could only find a bare ridge for fire position. The enemy were in vines and olive trees, and out-ranged the 40mm and 57mm guns completely at 2,000 yards. Five tanks were knocked out.'

In a word they had been ambushed.

Like all unseasoned troops the Allies were prone to unfounded reports, a disaster to CCB being brought about primarily because false rumours of an enemy advance led to a change of course in the dark into an uncharted bog: thus without a shot being fired eighteen tanks, forty-one guns and over 130 other vehicles were presented in running order to the

Left: Shermans – the key tank at El Alamein. *Above:* Tank debris at El Alamein, including Italian M13s and a solitary knocked-out Churchill – one of three on trial. *Below:* Brigadier-General Ernest Harmon, a tough US Armored Force leader

thankful Germans on the night of 10th December.

The war in Tunisia was reduced to a snarling scuffle amid winter rain-soaked mountains in the north, while the flowing mobile actions took place on the desert southern flank where it threatened the rear of the German-Italian Army withdrawing out of Tripolitania into the old French Mareth Line. Here 1st US Armored Division flexed its immature muscles and, under the direction of II US Corps Commander, General Fredendall, practised raids against the Axis to help gain battle experience of which it had next to none. The Axis were happy to oblige and all too soon showed that when it came to raiding they were the masters.

121

In January, taking a leaf out of the British book, the Axis attacked the weakest link in the Allied chain – the French – and having broken them, out-manoeuvred the Americans' armour for position to seize the Faid Pass. For a while 1st Armored beat the air between Faid and Gafsa, but matters did not come to a head until 14th February when, at Faid, out of the morning mist, four enveloping German battle groups swooped on a single US group – CCA with the infantry of 168th RCT watching from the nearby Djebel Lessouda – and in a matter of hours had netted the lot. It was not only the fact that control broke down in CCA (to such an extent that none of the artillery had been called upon to fire in support), nor that the Americans had been taken by surprise, which hurt; much more painful was the underlying peril of the cry by a distraught officer on Lessouda as he watched the débacle: 'I know panic when I see it.'

Worse was to follow, for panic is catching. Next day fifty tanks with armoured artillery and infantry from CCC rushed down from the north to rescue the isolated 168th RCT and restore the situation. Told, '. . . by fire and manoeuvre destroy the enemy armoured forces . . .' they charged against an enemy superior in numbers. But the Germans coolly shifted to positions on the flank to slaughter the Americans with well aimed fire while their machines did nothing other than plunge in a phalanx to destruction. Now the way was clear for the Germans to exploit the destruction of the Allied mobile reserve and it was nobody's fault but that of their General, von Arnim (who could not settle upon a firm strategy in consultation with Rommel when he joined hands from the south) that a more complete victory was not achieved. As it was, the last intact portion of 1st Armored Division (CCB) was brushed aside and, for a few days, Axis armour had a free run through the Kasserine Pass until brought to a halt by the combined efforts of part of 6th British Armoured Division and CCB under Brigadier Robinett on a line running through Thala and Bahiret Foussana.

The disruption of 1st US Armored Division in what is known as the Battle of Kasserine only went to underline how hopeless had been the inexperienced Americans' chances against seasoned troops of German calibre. In proportion to the British the expansion of the American Army had been much greater and swifter, and so imperfections and weaknesses were to be expected, particularly amongst a largely inexperienced officer corps. The local victory by CCB at Foussana helped restore self-respect and to no small extent this had been made possible by the personal leadership of Robinett in steadying his men, when the pressure came on, instead of allowing them to relapse into the unhealthy disease of precipitate withdrawal which had so cruelly infected the rest of the division.

It was now the job of General Patton, brought forward in haste, to put right what Fredendall had allowed to go wrong – and to do so in battle since already there was an immediate need for the Germans to be followed up where they retreated towards Gafsa and where they prepared to defend the Mareth Line. But mountainous country now meanly relegated the role of armoured forces to a lower degree of importance in relation to infantry and artillery.

When Rommel attacked Montgomery's Eight Army at Medenine on 6th March he lost over fifty tanks while the British lost none since their armour left the battle to artillery and anti-tank guns. In northern Tunisia succeeding tank attacks by von Arnim were stopped in dreadful going by British infantry and guns, and Patton's attempts to cut through to the coast via Maknassy towards the end of March broke down before well employed German guns holding commanding ground – to much the same pattern as when 1st US Infantry Division subsequently repulsed 10th Panzer Division when the latter tried to cut through to El Guettar. Similarly, when Montgomery tried to push tanks across the anti-tank ditch to help infantry storm the Mareth Line, they were wiped out by the Germans from stronger positions. Even the wide mechanised outflanking movement by the New Zealand Corps (joined later by 1st British Armoured Division) through the Dahar could only break out at Tebaga after the most enormous air and artillery bombardment had obliterated the few enemy who blocked the way. And again at Akarit, and along the length of the hills where Patton tried to hack his way to Sfax, only a deluge of fire and not a mass of armour prevailed when enemy dug in and fought back with confidence in their ability to kill tanks.

This was usually the way of it when little enough room was available to manoeuvre (such as the armoured forces invariably enjoyed in the limitless spaces of Russia). Yet where tanks could not go infantry could move only slowly at greater cost while standing in need of heavier volumes of artillery fire than ever to help clear the way. Stagnation such as had clogged the battlefields of the First World War had by no means set in, but the day when an inferior number of armoured formations would prevail in attack by the sheer dynamism of their presence had all but passed. Only once was Allied armour given the chance to fight a fully mobile battle in Tunisia, for as the Axis pulled back from Akarit and Maknassy at the beginning of April on their way to a last stand in the Tunisian bridgehead, it seemed that the 6th British Armoured Division might force the Fondouk Pass and seize the route centre at Kairouan, thus cutting off the entire mobile element of von Arnim's army. If that could have been done the Allied con-quest of Tunis and Bizerta would have been almost a formality. But General Alexander's orders to breach the pass were late in formulation, the force allocated to the job hurried in its preparations and the assault, when it took place, was mismanaged. American infantry, whose task it was to seize ground to the south of the pass, failed, for lack of leadership, to cross the start-line; British infantry who should have taken the vital ground to the north misunderstood an ambiguous order and did not bother to take the last essential hill. Determined to break-through at all costs the British Corps commander, General Crocker, ordered the 26th Armoured Brigade under 'Pip' Roberts to rush the pass, accepting such losses as mines and anti-tank guns would exact. The leading regiment was 17th/21st Lancers whose forebears had charged at Balaclava; instinctively they knew what was demanded and the remark of a squadron commander as he went to his death, 'Good-bye – we shall all be killed,' lent poignancy to the fatal occasion. At great loss in tanks – though, as in the nature of armoured warfare, not enormous casualties in men – the tanks charged and were duly smashed, though persevering with the demands of Roberts, who well knew the sacrifice he asked of his units, they broke through by nightfall. By then the opportunity to intercept the Axis had gone and the last grand opportunity for manoeuvre in Tunisia had passed.

What remained in North Africa was grinding mountain war throughout April and early May in the approaches to Tunis and Bizerta where British and American infantry strove bloodily to clear the way for one last drive by the armoured divisons. Here the British Churchill tanks scored many successes since they had the most astonishing agility and could climb what appeared to the Germans un-climbable slopes. Hence these tanks went where they were unexpected and scrambled to such heights that they

Above: Churchills in Tunisia. *Below:* Scourge of Allied armour – the German 88mm dual-purpose gun

could dominate the enemy from above as well as accompany the infantry who scaled alongside them. Here too French armour began to make its come-back, fighting in the grossly inadequate Somuas and Valentines given them by the British (for want of anything else), in bitter fighting near Pont-du-Fahs – and suffered in proportion to the inadequacy of the machines to the task. But in the last battles – when 1st US Armored Division roared out of the Tine Valley (known as the Mousetrap) toward Bizerta and the British 1st, 6th and 7th Armoured Divisions rolled down the Medjerda Valley to take Tunis and cut through the Cap Bon peninsula, the opposition had first always to be broken in the hills by infantry and overall by a furious and almost irresistible deluge of fire from artillery and aircraft before the tanks could bludgeon their way into the open. And in the midst of all a new phenomenon appeared – the phenomenon of the omnipotent Tiger which, when secure in a hide could, with its 88 and thick armour, hold up a whole squadron of tanks or even more for a quite disproportionate period.

These were the straws in the wind of the present which would blow up into the tempests of the future.

Hesitation

It had dawned only slowly upon the Allies that, although Operation Torch had liquidated a sizeable element of the German Army in Tunisia, it had also attracted an even greater proportion of the Allied armies to the same spot and there they now stood idle. Far from hastening the invasion of Northern Europe in 1943 the deflection of effort to North West Africa had effectively deferred that event until 1944 at the earliest. Thus, in order to maintain strategic momentum, the Allies were forced into invading the southern part of Europe – lands of mountain ranges, fast flowing rivers, citress fruit and olive groves where tactical momentum as expressed by mechanised forces was bound to be hampered as severely as it had been in Tunisia. The first steps – an invasion of Sicily in July – followed by landings on the mainland of Italy in September were primarily amphibious operations, of course; subsequently battles would be dominated by infantry supported by artillery and tanks. Only occasionally were the armoured divisions let off the leash, as when part of 2nd US Armored Division

enjoyed a few good runs against a withdrawing enemy in Western Sicily. More often than not the tank crews found themselves tied down to hard slogging in close country and once the battle had moved to Italy and the advance moved methodically up the leg of that complex land, the rhythm of progress was largely conditioned by erratic dashes from one river line to the next followed by bitter struggles for precipitous peaks in which the armour felt lucky if it moved at more than walking pace, and usually spent its time dodging up and down behind crests from fire position to fire position.

Jake Wardrop captured the atmosphere when he wrote from his driver's seat on one of those ephemeral occasions after the landing at Salerno when armour was let loose on its way to the River Volturno:

'The CLY had taken the lead and we followed on behind. The previous day the 1st Tanks had captured Cardito after a terrific scrap in which they lost eight Shermans of one squadron and six in another. They had pushed through the vineyards and bumped some well camouflaged SP guns.

They were very low and hard to spot in the trees; they are pretty bad medicine . . . We were now on the fields, cross-country stuff and it was raining. The going was heavy even for tanks and a number got stuck. Each troop of tanks took over a frontage of 400 yards and we were told that there was nobody in front but the Bosches. We spent the night in the turret, guns loaded and all keyed up for an attack that never came. Every tree appeared to move and I found myself about to open fire time and again.'

As the war slowed down in Italy before Cassino and later in the abortive bridgehead at Anzio, and as the Russians blunted the last great German attack at Kursk in July 1943 before plunging headlong towards the West, it became clear that only in Northern Europe would Allied armour pay the dividend for which so much capital had been invested. For a while after the victory in North Africa Allied progress seemed to hesitate as they paid feverish attention to preparations to invade Northern France through Normandy in the Spring of 1944. And during this lull there took place a great re-thinking about the future role of armour – a rethinking based upon the lessons learnt in the final stages of the North African campaign, on the beaches of Dieppe, Sicily and Salerno and upon the sort of fighting vehicles which would be available in 1944.

Close examination of battle performance revealed the need for revolutionary changes in organisation and this applied most forcibly to the Americans whose tank content was thought to be too high in relation to infantry and artillery. Consequentially the number of tanks was reduced by almost half to 186 mediums and eighty-three lights and the Combat Commands to two, each now normally comprising two tank battalions, an infantry battalion, an SP anti-tank company and an artillery battalion plus engineers and supporting services,

still leaving the division with a small combat reserve. The British, meanwhile, adhered to the balanced armoured divisional organisation settled upon in early 1942, but experimented with an extra armoured regiment for close reconnaissance purposes in place of the armoured car regiment which was extracted and put under Corps Command. The Mixed Divisions were dropped since they had proved unwieldy in practice as, with only two infantry brigades at his disposal, the divisional commander had only two options – to hold the front with two up (and no reserve) or one up and a wasted reserve equal to the committed force; moreover the single armoured brigade was not readily matched to the number of infantry formations and therefore was frequently wastefully mis-employed.

These reorganisations threw up several armoured formations for re-employment. With the Americans this was no great problem since they were still expanding and in the process of creating armoured divisions: by the end of the war they would have sixteen. The British, on the other hand, had reached the peak of their expansion and, due to shortage of manpower, were having difficulty in maintaining that level. In 1942 they formed their last new armoured division – the 79th and then, in 1943, the revised tendency to increase the infantry content of the army as a whole as well as in the armoured divisions themselves put the policy of 1940/1 into slow reverse. Soon armoured divisions themselves would have to be disbanded and, for instance, a number of trained RAC officers and men transferred to the infantry without the option.

Yet to suggest, as have some post war historians, that 'by 1943 the original concept of the Armoured Force had lost ground, its decisive role . . . played down and the official doctrine settled on the exploitation role' is misleading. The contemporary US War Department manual dealing

with the Employment of Armoured Units stated that three methods of attack could be used: –

1. Tanks in the initial assault, followed by other troops whose mission will be that of consolidating the position won ...

2. Foot soldiers making the initial assault followed by armored elements whose mission will be that of exploitation;

3. Tanks and foot troops together making the initial assault to reduce a hostile position.

And while the British gave precedence to the exploitation role in their manuals they were careful to point out that 'Cruiser tanks have, in recent operations, supported infantry divisions with marked success, and infantry tanks have, on at least one important occasion, carried out valuable work in a role usually allotted to cruisers.' The British made a perfectly correct interpretation of current battlefield experience when they laid down that, 'Only when the bulk of the hostile tanks have been destroyed will armoured formations attain such a measure of freedom and mobility as will enable them to exploit to the full their ability to inflict a decisive blow against the enemy's main forces.' Emphasis could only have been on the words, 'to the full', and this was inherent in their rejection in 1942 of a proposal by Martel that armoured divisions should be organised into groups of two; along with the Americans the British preferred to be flexible and to allocate divisions to corps in strict relation to the task in mind – and in Europe the mixture of infantry to armoured divisions more often than not settled in the proportion of two to one – as had been German practice in 1941!

In point of fact only the British could possibly have made this clear distinction between infantry and cruiser tanks since no other combatant nation gave official recognition

Return to Europe; US tanks in Sicily

to that technological dividing line. The British remained half convinced that if tanks were to accompany infantry in close combat they should be given priority in armoured protection above hitting power and speed. The Americans, meanwhile, worked on the assumption that one tank – for them the Sherman – could act both as cruiser and infantry tank, its nice combination of armour, hitting power and speed competing in combat worthiness with the worst that the enemy could do. Satisfied that Sherman in large numbers would outlast the war, they cancelled plans for Sherman's successor – the T20 – early in 1943 in order to concentrate on large scale Sherman production – and since no British cruiser was any better (except for the already obsolescent Cromwell) both had to make the best of the same bad job with Sherman. Far too late for the peace of mind of Allied crews, the Americans revived the T20 concept late in 1943 and the British, at about the same time, began to set up production of their A34. The former was to be produced as M26 (General Pershing) and would have a 90mm gun; the latter was to be a greatly improved Cromwell called Comet, with a 77mm gun: both were to go some way towards satisfying the demand for an all-purpose tank but neither could be ready until the end of 1944.

Significantly the concept of an all purposes main battle tank – the Capital tank – found strong favour with General Montgomery whose next task would be to command the Allied Forces during the landing and initial phase in Normandy. In theory he was right, but he did not appreciate the importance that hitting power was going to have when Shermans were opposed by the next generation of German tanks. Already Tiger had demonstrated its domination; soon Panther with an even better 75mm gun than that mounted in Mark IV and with frontal armour proof against the new British 76.2mm gun would be

roaming about in numbers. Against this only the 76.2mm gun in the Allied armoury would have the least chance of meeting the enemy on equal terms and therefore only by mounting this gun in a Sherman could the Allies have a hope of parity in the early stages of the invasion in 1944 since the latest American 76mm gun, with which they intended to up-gun their Shermans, was not nearly powerful enough.

Once again in 1943 the British Ministry of Supply played down the demand for up-gunning Sherman, but this time the army officers in the War Office had their way by circumventing the other Ministry just in time to get a few of the new Shermans (named Fireflys) converted by June 1944. Simultaneously the ammunition designers were able to achieve even better performance by the introduction of an entirely new type of shot, first for the 57mm and then for the 76.2. This was Armour Piercing

Above: Sicily: Shermans burned rather easily. *Right:* French armour is revitalised in North Africa

Discarding Sabot (APDS) in which the solid shot was carried in a jacket (or sabot) which fell off after the round had left the end of the muzzle. Because the sabot had a larger diameter than the projectile, greater initial force could be initially imparted and thus a markedly higher velocity achieved than if a lower pressure was applied to the base of the shot alone.

The introduction of bigger guns firing shot at higher velocities brought vexatious problems in their train, however. In order to be sure of hitting the enemy, a tank gunner was dependent upon his commander's ability, rather more than on his own, to detect the target and, above all, to estimate its range. Upon this data he could then align his telescope graticule upon the target and open fire. More often than not, because human error supervened, this resulted in a miss whereupon the gunner, if he had observed the fall of shot, could make corrections to his aim before firing again; dependent then upon the accuracy of his observations and corrections (and, not by any means least, his own coolness when in action) a· hit might be obtained with the second or subsequent shots. More powerful guns created clouds of smoke and debris when they were fired, however, and quite frequently this 'obscuration' would not have cleared in sufficient time to allow the crew to observe the path of the faster moving shot by its tracer or to see where the shot fell: thus data was frequently not available upon which to base corrections of aim. This was a common problem to Germans and Allies alike and one which they never fully resolved despite the most careful training in judging distance and also by constantly endeavouring to improve the quality of optical sights. In fact the Germans had better sights than the Allies – though only marginally so (and they paid for it by reason of their greater complexity and higher cost): the tactical differences were not therefore, enormous. Ironically, however, this technical problem reduced some of the tactical advantages of being able to penetrate the enemy at longer ranges, since the chances of scoring a hit remained better at shorter ranges at which the judging of range was easier.

With tactics there was also one notoriously largely unexplored area, closely associated with the ability or otherwise to see and hit the target, and that was in the art of night fighting. The American manual quoted above omits all reference to the technique, and though the British manuals gave it mention, they were reticent; one manual, rightly, declaimed on the difficulties involved – particularly in shooting since gunners could not see through telescopes

which did not admit enough light to enable them to distinguish the graticule of the cross wires – and concluded, 'A night attack by tanks will, however, be the exception not the rule.' Up to 1944 it had invariably been the practice for Allied tanks to move up behind the front at night in readiness for a dawn attack; the number of occasions on which they had deliberately driven in amongst the enemy could almost be counted on the figures of one hand. Movement had been undertaken by the light of searchlights shone on low cloud base and experiments had gone on in England and the Middle East with a powerful arc-light mounted behind armour in a tank turret. Two brigades of these latter, so-called CDL tanks were ready in early 1944 but their technique was so secret that hardly anybody knew how to employ them in battle. Night fighting therefore remained something of a black art in tank warfare, to be practised only in special circumstances when the moon was bright, the troops specially prepared and the enemy badly shaken.

Nevertheless, the pace of armoured warfare development was still increasing in 1943 and for that reason as much as any other it is ridiculous to suggest that the concept of an armoured force had lost momentum. Men had still to be carried safely through the beaten zone of machine-guns and high explosive shells; only armoured vehicles could do that and it was quite clear at the time that men on their feet were ever more loath to move forward on their own without tanks in close company. Nowhere was this problem likely to be of greater consequence than on the beaches of Northern Europe where German field defences, pillboxes and minefields had been skillfully integrated with natural barriers. For unprotected infantry to assail these would inevitably be costly no matter how efficacious the preliminary bombardment; the antidote could be found in an assault led by men behind armour equipped with special

Above: In Italy tanks are often little better than self-propelled artillery. *Right:* But in the towns the fighting is close and costly – notice the burnt out Sherman in the middle of this German position

devices to overcome each type of obstacle imposed by the defences. Already in existence in Britain were a number of devices, mostly in the primitive stages of development, which could be adapted to these purposes. They included DD, a swimming Sherman designed by Nicolas Straussler, driven by Duplex Drive propellers from the engine, the vehicle supported in the water by a canvas

screen attached to the hull which could be collapsed after landing from the sea; Crab, a mine sweeping tank based on Sherman, the improved version of flails used to detonate mines such as had first been tried at Alamein; AVRE, a converted Churchill tank developed by a Canadian called Denovan to overcome the sort of beach obstacles that had held back armour at Dieppe. This vehicle, armed with a short-range Spigot mortar which threw a twenty-five pound demolition charge (the Petard) could also transport bridges and fascines to cross or fill obstacles in addition to carrying other stores for a variety of demolition uses. There were a host of other special machines whose strange names ranged freely round the alphabet or were derived from the zoo.

In April 1943 this collection of oddities came under the command of Hobart whose 79th Armoured Division was among the first to be reduced because of manpower shortage. Under his imaginative drive the technical development of the special assault vehicles, the training of their crews and the creation of an assault technique to breach beach and landward defences was pressed with enormous vigour. With only a year in which to accomplish the task set by the CIGS, Brooke, he had to be ruthless not only in building assault teams and inculcating in them the spirit of the forlorn hope of siege assault parties of old, but also of persuading and bullying industry into making in haste what had not been made before. The success or otherwise of Hobart's labours could only be proved on the day of the invasion.

It must be recorded however that, although the Americans were offered an absolutely equal share in these special devices, they declined all but the swimming tanks – and gave as their reasons the difficulty of adapting their crews to British vehicles, and the fact that they could not see the need for such machinery on the beaches they were destined to assault.

In the case of the nationality of the equipment they were mistaken from the outset, for of the vehicles they rejected only the Churchill AVRE was not of American origin: of their tactical reasons only the results of the day could say if they had been wise.

Normandy was the place selected for the landings, and so it became one of the paradoxes of an invasion destined to be led and dominated by armour that the Normandy terrain was most unsuitable for armoured action. At the base of the Cotentin Peninsula where the Americans were to land, the exits from the beaches were either canalised by marshes or impeded by cliffs; further east, towards the mouth of the River Orne where the British would assault, the esplanade was of the popular seaside resort kind with villages and ribbon-developed villas providing ready-made centres for German resistance. Inland conditions became even more difficult since Normandy is distinguished by its Bocage – a system of minute fields, enclosed by thick double hedges and banks, and intersected by numerous narrow lanes connecting a plethora of small hamlets. Only the larger towns, Cherbourg, Carentan, St Lo, Bayeux, Caen and Falaise in the immediate vicinity of the invasion area, were linked by major roadways. Therefore the strategy of the campaign was likely to be conditioned by the need, once a lodgement had been achieved, to seize these main route centres as part of a policy aimed at building up a large administrative base sufficient to support a great battle. Tactics would be governed by the terrain – the open plain running south from Caen to Falaise providing the only arena where a large scale, untrammelled mobile battle by armoured forces might be fought, the rest of the bridgehead being bocage where an enemy on the defensive would have all the advantages of shooting back at short range from excellent cover and where armoured vehicles in crashing

Hobart's specialised armour. *Above:* Crab minesweeping flail
Below: Churchill AVRE with Spigot Mortar for concrete busting

Above: DD Sherman, first ashore on D-Day. *Below:* CDL, the one which was too secret

through and climbing over the hedges and banks could fatally expose the least well-armoured portion of their bellies. Since both German and Allied infantry now possessed a new kind of short-range anti-tank weapon – the bazooka type with a range of only one hundred yards but the capability with its hollow charge war head of blasting a hole through almost every known thickness of armour – tanks themselves were going to be in need of closer infantry protection against bazooka parties than ever before. Tactics, influenced by terrain, would thus dictate strategy since the massed employment of tanks accompanied by only a low infantry element could only take place south of Caen. Elsewhere, so long as the Germans could maintain a viable force in the bocage, they would have the distinct advantage of fighting a most economic defensive. It must be added, however, that although the Allies were aware of the existence of bocage and had been warned by the British (who had passed that way in 1940) of the difficulties it could raise, they did not recognise its defensive significance. Intent on making sure of getting ashore and then staying there, subsequent developments were pushed into the background.

In any case the Allied Army was committed to the most gigantic employment of armoured forces. The British contingent (which included a large Canadian element and the 1st Polish Armoured Division) produced five armoured divisions and eight independent armoured brigades – in all some 3,300 Shermans (of which barely one in twenty were Fireflys with the 76.2mm gun), Churchills and Cromwells backed up by sumptuous reserves of vehicles and trained crews. The United States Army was equally strong and ready to field six armoured divisions plus GHQ tank battalions for close co-operation with infantry divisions – making a total of something like 2,000 Shermans, of which an increasing number were being equipped with the 76mm gun and thicker frontal armour.

In addition, and appropriately enough on the eve of the invasion of France, French armoured divisions were due to make a re-entry in battle. After Operation Torch the slow rebuilding of the French Army to modern standards had gone forward at a steady pace and, apart from those French infantry divisions which had fought all along in Tunisia, a corps had also taken part in the fighting at Casino in the approaches to Rome in the Spring of 1944. Now, in North Africa, the French 1st Armoured Division was ready for operations and their 2nd Armoured Division, under General Leclerc, was preparing to follow the Americans to Normandy. They were manned by soldiers who wished to wipe out a disgrace, but their equipment was mainly from the United States as was their organisation. And with regard to their appearance a French historian could write of '. . . an Army whose uniforms were quite unfamiliar, since they had been heterogeneously derived from British and American models.' Unhappily the French Army was also divided within itself between the minority who had thrown in their lot with General de Gaulle and his Fighting French in 1940 and those who adhered to the Vichy regime until the Allies had come to North Africa. Though this caused tumultuous relations between the two factions over questions of tradition and promotion it did not greatly degrade fighting spirit – as was shown in Italy and as was soon to be tested in the home country.

On the morning of 6th June 1944 Allied armour led the way towards its greatest test. For the first time since the last battles in North Africa it was to be pitted against a mass of German armour with the prospect, if it could break out from the bocage, of treating the Germans to a drubbing as salutary as that inflicted by the Germans in 1940.

The deciding round

By the skin of their teeth the Allies got ashore in Normandy at dawn on 6th June (see Ballantine's Battle Book No 1), and this was not so much because the Germans resisted with accustomed vigour but because the rough seas, which had already caused one twenty-four hour postponement, were still making conditions extremely difficult in the approaches to the beaches. On the American sector the DD tanks had to be brought close to shore before launching at Utah beach to avoid the worst of the rough water, but these arrived with the infantry and had a profound effect in quelling the opposition. But at Omaha beach all but two of twenty-nine DDs were sunk by high seas – and the surviving pair were almost helpless throughout a day when the infantry spent several hapless hours pinned to the beach by severe German fire. Elsewhere at Omaha, when DDs were landed, the opposition was more quickly broken. On the British beaches most of the DDs arrived, either after a difficult swim or by beaching direct from their landing craft, and these were soon followed by the rest of 79th Armoured Division's flails and AVREs clearing a way for themselves, the infantry and the thousands of vehicles which would follow to attempt to drive deep inland. The battle was hard and the losses heavy, yet not nearly as heavy as they might have been if the armour had not been present at the outset. It was no coincidence, however, that the Americans lost forty-five men just clearing mines (without fighting) at Utah whereas the British on all three of their beaches, where the opposition was much heavier, lost only 169 at the same work throughout the whole day. The armoured, mechanised mineclearing devices were great preservers of lives.

It was well that the British did conquer their beaches with hardly a pause since it was against their sector, from out of the bocage-free ground in the vicinity of Caen, that the preponderance of German armour would counter-attack. Indeed, no sooner had the commander of 21st Panzer Division come to understand the nature of the British threat than his units were on their way to the coast, and throughout that hectic day it was this division alone of German armour which struggled with British and Canadian tanks infiltrating inland at the head of the assault infantry divisions. Shielded by the bocage the Americans were spared an immediate head-on collision with panzer divisions and were given time to gather themselves together after the initial set-backs. On D plus 1 Cromwells from the leading British armoured division – the 7th, brought home from the Mediterranean – were coming ashore, hoping to assemble north of Bayeux to exploit an advance by 8th Armoured Brigade with 50th Division deep into the bocage at Villers Bocage. Instead 7th Armoured found itself engaged in local operations to clear out enemy on the western flank to give assistance to the Americans at Omaha, and it was not until 10th June that this division was given its first opportunity to cut loose.

At once 7th Armoured Division's tanks and infantry became embroiled in the sunken lanes and tiny fields where, ironically, the short 75mm gun was easier to traverse than the long 75s on the Panthers they were beginning to encounter. But it was the lorried infantry brigade which was most needed, though since it had not come ashore until 12th June the division as a whole was delayed in asserting its full power. Nevertheless it was by manoeuvre (even in such close country) that the armour found a gap in the German defences on 13th June and stormed into Villers Bocage, sending a column of tanks and half-tracks in a hook to the east to take the Germans at Caen in rear. And then a Tiger tank demon-strated how hopeless was the Cromwell's task, for a single one of these tough opponents, effortlessly defeating shot from the British 75s even at short range, took its time and shot the whole British column – twenty-five armoured vehicles all told – into a blazing shambles. The range of engagement was never more than 800 yards – about the maximum of any shooting in the bocage; but let it be clearly understood that, when on the defensive, Allied armour against German counter attacks, the latter suffered casualties which were quite as disastrous as those incurred by the former.

And so it went on into July, with furious fighting for small gains and painful losses. Compared with dynamic success in Italy, where the Cassino defences had at last been broken and Rome had fallen on 4th June, the stalemate in Normandy began to look a waste of effort particularly to those who reflected that the Italian front took low priority and that it was in Normandy where every Allied hope was pinned. Tank losses were high and infantry losses higher still. The Bazooka became a bogey at short range and where longer ranges were obtainable to the south of Caen, the German 75s and 88s imposed a check with their old terror. To the tank crews it might well have been demoralising had not the vast Allied preponderance in artillery and air-power compensated for the disparity in tank gun power. The fallibility of superior numbers against superior fire was now exposed – for when one Tiger could stave off a squadron of Shermans, Churchills or Cromwells (as often occurred) the matter of ratio became meaningless. Not that artillery or air-power actually knocked out so many tanks: all the former could do was make life unpleasant for them and cause them to shift position while, at the same time, slaughtering unarmoured troops; all the latter could do was isolate the battlefield and deprive the Germans of supplies – above all of fuel.

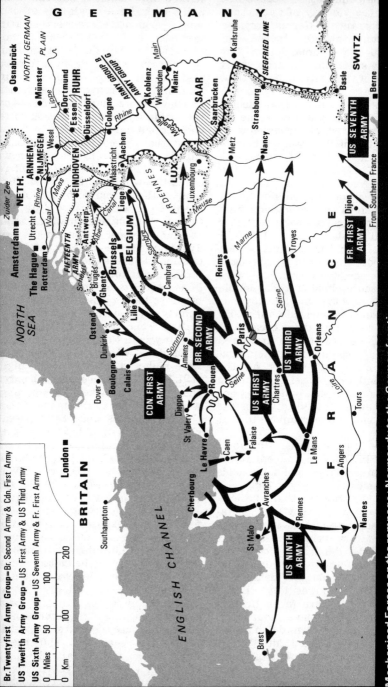

Mechanised Forces on the rampage : Normandy to the German frontier

Key:
Br. Twentyfirst Army Group = Br: Second Army & Cdn. First Army
US Twelfth Army Group = US First Army & US Third Army
US Sixth Army Group = US Seventh Army & Fr. First Army

Nevertheless in a memorandum written early in July by Montgomery, he failed to indicate grave dissatisfaction with the quality of his armour, even though the matter was the subject of complaint in the newspapers and on the floor of the British House of Commons. '. . . we have had no difficulty in dealing with German armour once we had grasped the problem,' he wrote, and went on to claim that the 76.2mm gun compared favourably with any of the German weapons and that the 57mm APDS would penetrate the Panther anywhere except on the sloping front plate. But he begged the question: the single troop of Sherman Fireflys in each squadron of tanks could not be everywhere with their 76.2mm gun and the Panther rarely exposed anything other than its frontal plate to attack; moreover the Tiger, as Montgomery admitted, and as had long been known, was superior to anything the Allies had. It is probable that Montgomery did no more than assess the performance of his armour at short ranges in the close bocage and that his memorandum was an attempt to help the British War Office stave off mounting public discontent arising from bad publicity. South of Caen on 18th July, however, and the fundamental weaknesses of the Shermans and Cromwells were fully exposed in a battle which came about purely as the continuation of Montgomery's basic strategy, which aimed at making General Dempsey's Second British Army fight to contain German armour on the eastern flank of the bridgehead while General Bradley's First US Army attacked south from St Lo to effect the decisive breakout where the enemy held thinnest. But on 10th July, after ferocious battles in the hedgerows, First Army had been fought to a standstill and, moreover, had attracted German armour against itself away from Caen. Hence Dempsey suggested that the British should now make a southerly breakout from Caen – a solution speedily rejected

by Montgomery who nevertheless realised that a renewed British effort was required in order to bring the Germans back, close to Caen, prior to the next American attempt. This operation was to be called 'Goodwood' and, in the words of Montgomery's operation order was, in essence, 'To engage German armour in battle and "write it down" . . .' In amplification Montgomery said that three armoured divisions – 7th, 11th and Guards – 'will be required to dominate the area Bourguebus – Vimont – Bretteville . . .' but he was careful to play down any prospect of achieving a breakout. The use of armoured divisions to make the breach on their own was not merely an acknowledgement of their capability to do so – it was also dictated by information from London that the bottom of the infantry manpower barrel was being scraped and that while there were plenty of tanks and · their crews to spare, infantry would have to be conserved if the British Army was to continue as a viable force.

Thus the scene was set for the greatest ever confrontation between German and Allied armour in a confined space (on average the battle arena was to be only 8,000 yards across), for in addition to the three British armoured divisions with over 700 tanks plus one hundred self-propelled anti-tank guns there was the armour assisting four other infantry divisions operating on either flank plus flails and AVREs – a grand total of some 1,350 armoured vehicles plus a mass of other transport. Against this concentrated mass the Germans would be able to send four panzer divisions – say some 300 armoured vehicles backed up by seventy-eight 88mm guns, 194 field guns and 272 *nebelwerfer* multiple rocket launchers. But the Germans enjoyed two other invaluable advantages: they had devined that an attack of these dimensions might well take place on this ground (for want of anywhere else) and they had deepened their defences to ten miles, holding the key villages as local fortresses around which their armour would manoeuvre to open fire from concealed positions.

After over 2,000 Allied bombers had soaked the corridor through which the armour was to advance, the tanks drove into the clouds of dust kicked up by the awe-inspiring bombardment, to find themselves amongst an enemy who was stunned. But although the opening moves went well, 'battlefield grit' was already applying friction. Minor obstacles in the way of the leading tanks slowed down the advance which, in consequence, fell behind the artillery barrage, with the result that the surviving Germans farther back were able to come into action and amplify the British delay – delay which gave all the more time for the alerted panzer divisions to move to their pre-arranged battle positions on Bourguebus Ridge. Meanwhile, in the British rear, the Guards Armoured Division was finding great difficulty in crossing the River Orne by the relatively few bridges. Already a suffocating traffic jam was building up which, throughout the remainder of the battle, would hamper the flow into action of fresh units.

On the gentle northern slope of Bourguebus Ridge the main forces of armour came into collision and it was there that British armour rather than the Germans' was 'written down.' Mark IVs, Panthers and Tigers came into action alongside a deadly line of 88s, the open country fogged by dust and smoke was streaked with the tracer flash of armour piercing shot and dappled with the flare from burning tanks as first the Shermans of 11th and Guards and then the Cromwells of 7th Armoured Division became jammed and almost stationary in a tank charnel house bounded by Bras, Grenthville, Cagny and Bourguebus. At the end of the day the British had lost almost 140 tanks from their armoured divisions alone – the disabled vehicles struck over and over again when the German gunners failed to discriminate the living from the dead. Vitally important, the Germans held the ridge having lost little ground to their opponents, and after another three days exchange the line rested only a few hundred yards in advance of the position reached on the first day, while some 200 tanks had been lost from the British armoured divisions alone plus many others on the flanks, with the infantry divisions. Moreover, infantry casualties in the subsidiary attacks had been much higher than among the armoured divisions – yet another sharp reminder of the economy in lives which armour effected. Possibly one of the main lessons rubbed into the British was the need to adopt flexible battle groups similar to those which worked so well within the American Combat Commands. On the first day of Goodwood the three armoured regiments in each armoured brigade had lost momentum because their single battalion of armoured infantry was insufficient to the task while the lorried infantry brigades had been kept too far in rear and had lacked adequate tank support when committed to battle on their own. From now on the Armoured and Lorried Infantry Brigades would be regrouped so that each included elements from the other in similar style and proportion to the American system.

By 21st July seven of the nine panzer divisions had been attracted to the British front and only two with a few emaciated infantry formations were left to face First US Army. The American attack, called 'Cobra,' should have gone in that day, but due to bad weather had to be postponed until the 24th. When at last it did roll forward through the bocage behind a terrific weight of high explosive, there was practically nothing to stop three corps, each with its armoured division – a mass of armour accelerating with ever increasing weight and panache into a vacuum. This was the breakout at last – a

Above: Specialised armour leads the invasion – flail, AVRE, bulldozer, and a DD in the lead – while the infantry hug the beach. *Below:* The tank/infantry team in Normandy

Above: Shermans versus Tiger in the bocage.
Above right: Breakout in Normandy. *Below:* Slogging match

flood of armour coursing irresistibly where it liked (led incidentally by tanks carrying steel blades welded in front to cut holes through the steep banks) and soon to be joined by the mass of Patton's Third Army, fresh into battle for the first time, by British armoured divisions brought round from Caen to widen the gap already torn by the Americans and by a complementary night assault down the Caen–Falaise road, by armour and infantry, followed next day by the 4th Canadian and 1st Polish Armoured Divisions. The entire assembly of Allied armour in France was in motion at once, several thousand armoured vehicles heaving southward and then curling round to the east to envelop and pursue an utterly shattered enemy. For even when the Germans struck back at the American flank at Mortain, it was to no avail: a pause they might inflict on the flank-guard provided by 3rd US Armored Division along with some consternation at divisional level, but in the higher echelons there grew a feeling of satisfaction that, instead of escaping while there was time, the Germans were digging their own grave in the bocage.

The victory of Normandy was consecrated to the south of Falaise where American armoured pincers,

moving in a short hook from the south linked up with the British battering down from the north while the mass of Patton's armour split in two, some going westward into Brittany and the rest roaring eastward in a wild plunge to the Seine. This is not the place to describe the breakout and pursuit in detail (see *Breakout*, Campaign Book No 4). Only miniatures can be painted as part of a vast canvas – such as the drama of the taking of Paris with Leclerc's 2nd French Armoured Division brought forward to lead and do the honours for France; the fresh Allied landings in Southern France and the drive to the north by American and French 1st Armoured Division – the latter moving with fantastic speed until it linked up fervently with Leclerc at Chatillon-sur-Seine on 12th September; and the all consuming dash with which the American armour, once free from the constrictions of the bocage, rolled through France until the last drop of petrol had run out. Yet the actual day by day advances were always erratic; at times sixty miles might be covered and then there would have to be a pause either to allow fuel supplies to catch up, or to overcome some local centre of German resistance and net a horde of prisoners, or to wait for some delayed flanking formation to come

Above: Leclerc enters Paris
Right: Major-General Maurice Rose
Far right: Cromwell in Brussels

alongside. Indeed, although Patton's Third Army made very dramatic progress and its ebullient leader generated waves of propaganda, its progress was little better than that of its neighbours. At times, it is true, his Army Group commander, General Bradley, had to hold him back for strategic reasons, but First US Army, now under General Hodges, showed that despite the fatigue induced by fighting in the bridgehead (which Third Army had not had to endure) it could move quite as fast when in pursuit of a broken enemy – and gather emotional honours such as when 3rd and 7th Armored Divisions entered Chateau Thierry almost simultaneously and revived memories of American glory in the First World War.

The most sustained and fastest pursuit of all was made, however, by the British 11th and Guards Armoured Divisions in General Horrocks's Corps when, between 30th August and 4th September, they advanced 340 miles from the River Seine to Antwerp (including one dramatic march by moonlight on 30th/31st August when it raced ahead forty miles to capture Amiens and a German Army commander), finishing up by interning 6,000 Germans in the Antwerp zoo for want of other secure accommodation.

In this wildly satisfying period when each nationality competed with the other to win laurels, one particularly strong characteristic of Allied tank design came forcibly to notice: outgunned they might be, but they could at least motor long distances without breaking down in large numbers. Both Shermans and Cromwells, able to maintain average speeds of twelve miles per hour, kept going for hun-

running enemy time to organise a coherent resistance along a continuous front. In movement the Allied armour had shown its superiority over the Germans; in a positional war the tables might be turned.

The key to the matter was fuel which still had to be shipped over Normandy's beaches or through the artificial Mulberry harbour at Arromanches and then driven in trucks along tenuous supply routes an ever increasing distance to the front. An immediate shortening of the lines of communication and an improvement of deliveries depended upon the capture of the Channel Ports and the subjugation of the Germans who held the approaches to Antwerp. But Montgomery's Army Group was more fully committed to a drive into Germany than to taking the ports on his flank, and though these operations were begun by First Canadian Army on 10th September (and absorbed several infantry divisions, a great many armoured brigades and much specialised armour in heavy fighting amongst the best defended sectors of the Atlantic Wall) it was not until 20th November that the first merchant ship was able to enter Antwerp docks. Until then the Allied mechanised armies had to thrive on a sparse supply of every sort of commodity.

In the middle of September all the fronts contracted remorselessly upon the German frontiers, but only one cut a deep incision. That incision was where Montgomery attempted to pierce the German frontier to the north of the Siegfried Line by air-landing troops on the bridges over the rivers at Grave, Nijmegen and Arnhem and linking them up by a thrust from Guards Armoured Division as the forerunner of a great drive eastwards towards Munster. At first the momentum of this advance seemed set for all its objectives on time, for the Guards were in Eindhoven and only five miles south of Nijmegen by dusk on the first day. Moreover the Germans had

dreds of miles on end and even if the units which swept across France and Belgium, to arrive on the frontiers of Holland and Germany in the first week of September, were tired and desperately short of fuel, they were at least almost complete. That was something which could not have been said about the German tanks had they been put to the same test, for the Panthers and Tigers still broke down all too easily.

Throughout this period the great debate surrounding General Eisenhower's demand for a broad front drive into Germany and Montgomery's case for a single, narrower thrust into the North German plain conditioned all other considerations. The underlying considerations were logistics and a mutual desire to maintain momentum, but this meant keeping up supplies so that the armour would not need to stop and thereby give the

nothing immediately available to reinforce the enfeebled troops they already had in the area, and therefore had the Guards made one supreme effort to drive on to Nijmegen that night, instead of halting, they might have joined the American paratroopers on the bridge that night or, at latest, early next morning. As it was the Guards halted after a tough day's fighting, and by the time they reached Nijmegen next day the Americans, fully absorbed by German counter-attacks, could spare little else to help take the bridge and cross the river. This was unfortunate, for if British armour could have crossed the River Waal early that day it might have had a free run to Arnhem where the 1st British Airborne Division had possession of the north end of the bridge over the River Lower Rhine. It would never again be so easy, and indeed the airborne adventure was to founder because armour could not be brought to the leading paratroopers' assistance.

In fact, for several months, a sort of stalemate was to freeze the northern front broken only by skirmishes, for in the flat, low lying land amongst the rivers, tanks could not move with freedom and were prey to anti-tank guns firing at long-range, while in the more enclosed country sheltering the fortifications of the Siegfried Line, where they stretched south to the Swiss frontier, the defences coalesced in stubborn defiance. Against flood and amongst waterlogged fields only special vehicles, such as the US Buffalo, could be fully mobile, and so operations became more often than not direct, with little scope for wide outflanking movements: against pill-boxes AVREs again came into their own with their Petards and were complemented by flame-throwing tanks, while the ordinary gun tanks helped subdue the other enemy opposition round and about. In this close fighting the bazooka type weapons seemed to pose an even greater threat than the conventional anti-tank guns and mines, for by

now there were immense numbers available to the Germans, many of whom were ready to sacrifice themselves at short range when firing a weapon which was anything but reliable. Tank crews who had been 88, Tiger and Panther conscious for years now became bazooka obsessed at a time when the end of the war looked close in sight and therefore when undue risks were not readily taken. Tank crews spent long hours thickening their armour by welding track plates on the outside. Not only were the infantry as tardy as ever to advance without tanks in company, tanks were now reticent about going far without a close infantry escort to 'winkle out' bazooka parties. Force majeure had effected an amalgamation between men on foot and men behind armour such as the Generals had failed to achieve with their paper schemes.

Christmas was coming and with it, as a tardily delayed present, many more Shermans with the 76mm gun, the new Pershing with its powerful 90mm gun, and the Comet with its 77. On the British side specialised armour was being readied again for the day when it might have to lead a crossing of the River Rhine. With quickening impulse great dumps of stores were being built up to support Allied armour, infantry and artillery on their last campaign against Hitlers' Reich – and those who could spare a thought for other theatres of war knew that, in Italy, the slow crawl up that peninsula was almost in sight of its last bound as well.

Meanwhile those who believed that they might have to go and fight the Japanese when Germany was done, took encouragement from news of Japanese defeats by the Americans in the Pacific and in Burma where a Japanese Army had been defeated by the British on the frontiers of India. The islands and the jungle were certainly no place for armour to dominate, but Buffalo type vehicles could always be found in the forefront of the landings from the sea, and then they would be followed by Shermans brought in to blast pill-boxes before the US infantry put in the final assault. And in these grim battles, where the 'front' was often just one tank wide, the tank crews had to deal with almost every sort of hazard known to their friends in Europe, plus the possibility of a Japanese sitting in a hole with a bomb to blow up himself and the tank at the right moment. Only in Burma did an armoured formation ever enjoy a free run in something like the European manner, when on the advance past Mandalay and towards Rangoon, General Slim was to swing mechanised formations about in the grand manner. Nevertheless the sort of description Slim once wrote of a typical jungle assault by tanks and infantry was representative almost anywhere in the world in thick country:

'A single Sherman tank, in a scrub-topped hollow, lay between us and the spinney . . . In the intervals of firing we could hear its engine muttering and grumbling. The dispositions of our forces, two platoons and one tank, were plain enough to us but I could see no enemy. Then the tank revved up its engine to a stuttering roar, edged forwards a few yards, fired a couple of shots in quick succession, and discreetly withdrew into cover again. I watched the strike of shot. Through my glasses I could see, about five hundred yards away, three low grassy hummocks . . . Straining my eyes I spotted a dark loophole in one, around which hung the misty smoke of a hot machine-gun . . . The tank intervened again. Without shifting position it lobbed two or three grenades and a white screen of smoke drifted across the front of the bunkers. One of the Gurkhas below us sprang to his feet, waved an arm, and the whole party, crouching as they went ran forward . . . As the fight drew to its climax . . . the tank reappeared round the spinney's flank and advanced still shooting. Gradually it worked to the rear of the bunkers, and suddenly we were in its

Lee in Burma

line of fire with overs ricochetting and plunging straight at us . . . After this little excitement : . . . we watched the final stages of the action. The fire of the Brens and rifles swelled in volume; the tank's gun thudded away. Suddenly three Gurkhas sprang up simultaneously and dashed forward. One fell, but the other two covered the few yards to the bunkers and thrust Tommy guns through the loopholes.'

An almost perfect example of infantry tank co-operation, emulating a thousand and more small engagements which made up the whole mighty conflict then coming to its climax from one end of the world to the other. Soon the opposition would be engulfed by armour, but there was one last great clash to come.

Finale and future

Looked at in retrospect there is something rather pathetic about the last great offensive launched by the German Army into the Ardennes on 16th December 1944. Probably it was the sheer incredibility of it that most caught the Americans holding that front by surprise and threw them off balance for the first few days, and because it was their infantry divisions which held that attenuated front, it was they who suffered most at the start. VIII Corps, which covered almost the entire front under attack, had only the comparatively inexperienced 9th Armored Division in reserve and inexperienced divisions are best blooded in their own time and not in a state of crisis. But though this battle was to develop in country so enclosed as to prescribe free mobility, and on roads so icy as to make that eventuality even less likely, the over-cast condition of the sky at least gave the Germans an opportunity to deploy their armour unimpeded except by Allied ground forces. Thus the Americans found themselves face to face with ground troops alone, having to rely upon their own unaided skill at arms for salvation. With twenty eight divisions (nine of them panzer) Hitler could throw into action the greatest concentration of force achieved by the Germans since two

years past, and though the proficiency of the soldiers was neither so keen nor polished as in 1940, the armoured vehicles were individually much more powerful, even if the resources to maintain their sustained effort were not to be found. They were to give the American Army its supreme test.

The battle which raged to its climax on 23rd December when, at last, the weather cleared and Allied air-power was able to intervene massively to complete the soldiers task, will not be described here in detail. Typical of the experience of many US formations was that of 3rd Armored Division whose CCB roared into action on the northern flank of the Bulge on 18th December near Eupen against enemy paratroops, and then found itself up against 1st SS Panzer Division. Ironically, and from the start, the Americans were forced into distributing their combat commands as a stiffener amongst the infantry rather as the French had done as a matter of course with their tanks in 1940, but the Americans did not make the same mistake as the French by just distributing the tanks along the line. The combat commands fought as teams which mostly moved rapidly from one point of danger to another, coming into action concentrated to secure one piece of ground after another and thereby giving invaluable indirect support to the hard pressed infantry divisions.

Major-General Maurice Rose, the commander of 3rd Armored, and perhaps the best of all the American tank leaders, only thought in terms of offence. When told to secure the Manhay to Houffalize road, he attacked with his sole available combat command into the mass of the enemy until this unit could move no further. One detachment commander, trapped in Marcouray, replied to the German who asked him to surrender with, 'If you want this town come right in and take it.' He was still there until ordered to break out four days later. CCA now joined Rose and was reinforced by elements from outside the division while engineers were improvised as infantry when the German drive was intensified. At Amonines, on Christmas eve, the last great enemy attempt was made to overcome this stubborn division and, to quote their history, 'Cooks, drivers and maintenance men went into the line. Tankers who had lost their Shermans in the furious fighting, went up to dig foxholes and wait with the "Blitz Doughs" . . . The enemy tried a frontal assault with tanks and suffered heavily. He tried tanks and infantry combined: they didn't work. He came back screaming mad in an infantry envelopment – and was slaughtered in hundreds by the grim defenders. Supported by mortars, artillery and rocket fire, the German attack surged forward twelve separate times – and twelve times it went reeling back in confusion leaving mounds of dead on the new snow'. It was the moment of crisis – a crisis repeated all along the front as British armour began to arrive at the Meuse after the American epic had killed the German offensive. The defensive victory had been an American one. From now on nearly all the last victories would be theirs as refreshed and omnipotent they turned to counter-attack with a full blooded offensive led by their own armour.

It would be entirely misleading to give an impression that the rest of the campaign in North-West Europe was a walk-over. Stiff fighting remained to be done and the ground between the German frontier and the Rhine would exact severe penalties before that river had been reached and crossed in strength. Throughout a hard winter Allied armour gradually regained the initiative by attacks in Alsace, in the Ardennes, along the River Roer and through the Reichswald Forest. But a standard pattern became quite clear after the turning point in the Ardennes. There the last German central reserve had been reduced to impotence: from now on their armour would be dispersed and overborne by a mass of Allied armour – Russian tanks pouring in across the eastern frontiers, British, American and French from Italy in the south and France, Belgium and Holland in the west. Moreover that Allied armour was at last receiving tougher tanks which could stand up to the Panthers and Tigers – the Pershing and the Comet beginning to replace vehicles which had been outclassed for over a year.

The tempo of the war moved quicker, a smaller price had to be paid for each slice of German territory and as the fronts loosened, the bullying characteristic inherent in tank forces supervened. Short jabs by combined teams gradually gave way to free-ranging thrusts in which the tanks took more risks at less cost, and pushed on without quite the same dependence on infantry as escorts. On the maps the arrow heads representing each day's advance got longer and the reports recorded a flood of events which swamped each other by sheer drama.

Hard fighting to the east of Nijmegen drew the local German reserves against the British and left great gaps for the Americans to penetrate in the direction of the River Rhur and Cologne. Suddenly American armoured divisions were debouching freely towards

Above: US armour enters Germany at Aachen. *Below:* The Germans' last fling in the Ardennes – a Panther burns. *Above right:* Third Army drives on. *Below right:* Over the Rhine

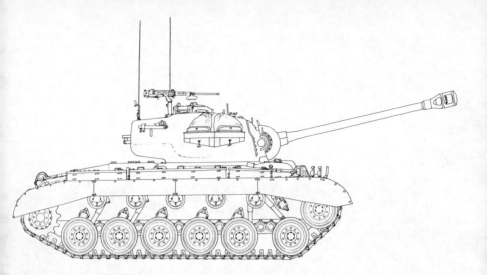

The new generation. US M26 (Pershing) – a much needed replacement for the Sherman. *Weight:* 42 tons. *Armour:* 145mm. *Armament:* 1 × 90mm and 3mgs *Speed:* 30mph. *Range:* 90 miles. *Crew:* 5

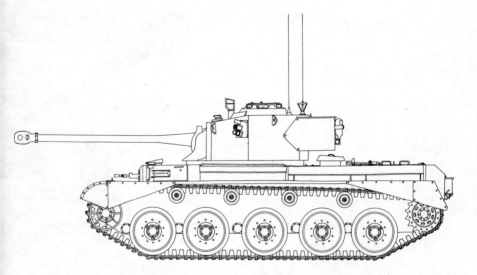

Comet – best British tank of the war. *Weight:* 34 tons. *Armour:* 101mm *Armament:* 1 × 77mm and 2mgs. *Speed:* 30 mph. *Range:* 120 miles. *Crew:* 5

the river with bridges being blown up in their faces wherever they appeared. Then on 7th March the leading tank and infantry platoons of 9th Armored Division's CCB arrived on the high ground overlooking the railway bridge at Remagen and to their astonishment saw that not only was it still intact, but that the Germans were still crossing over to the other bank. The infantry at once started to advance stealthily under cover across country in an effort to arrive unseen at the bridge, then the tanks were sent in a mad rush to carry on when the infantry got held up. But as they reached the west end of the bridge the charges were exploded, the bridge seemed to lift – and then it settled, weakened but intact: the charges had failed. What followed describes exploitation at its best: infantry rushed over supported by heavy fire from the tanks; engineers dashed after them cutting every wire in sight to prevent further demolition; reinforcements were flung across and fanned out on the other side until by nightfall a bridgehead had been established on the eastern bank supported by a curtain of artillery fire which no amount of enemy counter-attack could penetrate. An armoured division had achieved cheaply, with dash, what a mass of other formations were to essay deliberately elsewhere at much greater cost – and it is possible that no other escapade at this period of the war symbolised better the inherent economy of armoured forces.

What followed, as the Allied armies streamed across Europe's greatest water barrier on a front the length of the frontier itself, brought the war to its foregone conclusion in a torrent of armoured thrusts. Even infantry divisions climbed aboard tanks and advanced with the same sustained pace as armoured divisions. Germany was cut to ribbons until the Western Allies met the Russians on the Elbe. This was a period of immense triumphs interlaced with little tragedies – the swinging advances by the armoured divisions brought only rarely to a halt by local German resistance, which, nevertheless exacted the last futile killings with so little else to be achieved; the deep advance by Rose's 3rd Armored Division east of the Ruhr – ninety miles in one day – and the tragic death of its commander a few days later in an ambush; the dramatic thrust of Patton's Third Army across the frontiers of Czechoslovakia; the arrival of American armour in the Brenner Pass from Italy and of the British in Venice, until at last the whole German façade crashed to the ground and the tanks stood still, their guns and tracks silent at last.

As the last shots were being exchanged between Allied and German armour five tarpaulined shapes were being hastily carried by ship and then tank-transporter across Europe to the fast disintegrating battlefront. Beneath the tarpaulins was Britain's latest tank – the Centurion – rushed through production in an effort to try it out in combat before the war ended. Here was a fighting vehicle which revealed that the British had caught up to the pre-eminent position in tank design which she had lost at the beginning of the war – a forty seven ton vehicle armed with a 76.2mm gun, plus a 20mm cannon, with a speed of twenty three miles per hour and sloped frontal armour 120mm thick – more than twice the thickness of the original and once invulnerable Matilda I. This was a tank which, had it the chance, could have met and defeated the best that the Germans possessed and was superior too to the latest American Pershing which had already proved itself in combat. It was the irony of the situation that Britain had at last produced a machine worthy of her crews when the need seemed past.

But it was even more ironic that, as the war, which had been fought at the beck and call of armour, came to an end, the soldiers of both the British and American armies began to throw doubt upon armour's future at war. In

Above: A Comet runs the last leg of the tank war. *Below:* Germany burns
Above right: The last assault. *Below right:* Tailpiece

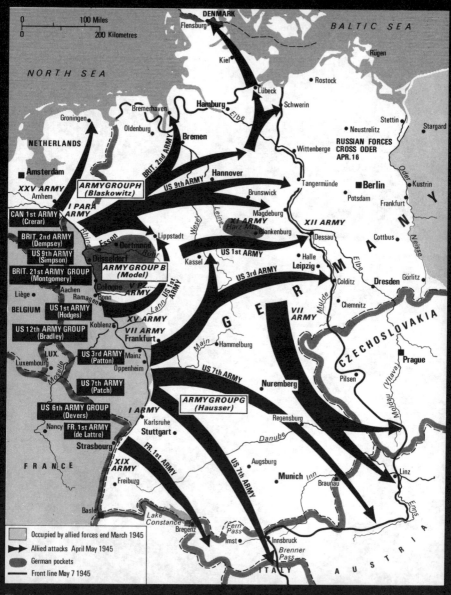

The final moves

much the same way as the pundits of mid war years had foretold the demise of the tank in the face of high-velocity anti-tank guns, those who set out to prophesy the future of atomic war in 1945 foretold the decline of the tank in the face of hollow charge missiles such as bazookas. They certainly digested the lessons of the last battles in which armour had been inhibited by well developed anti-tank defences, but they also forgot that tanks, armoured infantry and artillery carriers had met and overcome a succession of threats by evolving new methods and techniques of their own, and that the atomic threat posed an entirely novel situation. There will always be the wail of pessimists who clearly envisage every hazard without at the same time remembering that each hazard creates a challenge and an antidote. If nothing else, those who said that armoured vehicles would be swept from the battlefield rarely suggested what might be the substitute if warfare was to continue (as there was every sign in 1945 that it would) and stagnation of the First World War variety avoided.

Towards the end of the Second World War hardly a single action was fought in which armoured vehicles did not play a part. The reason for this was simple. It was essential for men to be protected by some sort of cover if they were to move across battlefields which were invariably swept and made uninhabitable by a dense volume of small-arms and shell-fire. Armoured vehicles played their part in proportion to the track bearing quality and density of the country in which they operated. Where the going was good, in open country, more armoured vehicles could be employed and, indeed, *had* to be employed to ensure a decision. Where the ground was soft and the terrain extremely close, as in jungle, men on their feet might make progress until blocked by some impregnable position, but then the next quick step forward depended on an armoured vehicle being dragged up to clear the way. As a rough rule of thumb the proportionate need of a single vehicle in jungle might be equal to and absorb the same effort as the deployment of a squadron on the plains: yet both were vitally important.

Allied armour had spent most of the war in adversity – either outnumbered when the equal of its foes in quality, or inferior in quality when actually outnumbering the enemy. Sheer numbers, in the end, were probably the decisive factor, but the needless losses incurred in sacrificing quality to numbers are no credit to those whose vacillating policies had permitted such a situation to arise. To tax the goodwill and lives of the crews for doctrinaire reasons by allowing genuine research into the future to be clouded and prevented by subjective reasoning, could be tantamount to an undervaluation of human dignity. It was the good fortune of the Allied leadership and industry that there were soldiers in the field whose determination in action could make up for technical deficiencies in defeating an enemy who was every bit as skilful and brave as – and usually better equipped than – themselves.

In 1945, as the war came to an end, thoughts of a war of the future were muted, yet one thing those who cared were determined to ensure, and that was that the examination of new trends in tactics and technology should not be allowed to atrophy as they had by a previous generation. So long as there was a threat of violence, research and development had to be continued into a war the like of which no man could imagine. It could not be doubted, however, that mechanisation would continue to expand, as it had expanded in the Second World War, using armoured fighting vehicles whose striking power would be persistently enhanced and whose means of protection might also be improved. If there had to be a cold war there would have to be armies, and if the Allies were to survive they had to have armour.

Bibliography

A History of the 17th/21st Lancers 1922-1959 RLV ffrench Blake (Hamish Hamilton, London. MacMillan, New York)
Memoirs of a Unconventional Soldier JFC Fuller (Nicholson & Watson, London)
Vers Armée le Métier C de Gaulle
Memoirs of War: The Call to Arms 1940-1942 C de Gaulle (Collins, London)
The French Army: A military-Political History Paul-Marie de la Gorce (Weidenfeld & Nicolson, London. Braziller Inc, New York)
North West Africa: Seizing the Initiative G Howe (Dept of the US Army, Washington, DC)
Battle History of the First Armoured Division G Howe (Dept of the US Army, Washington, DC)
The Tanks Basil H Liddell Hart (Cassell, London. Praeger, New York)
Abbeville 1940 J Marat (Durassié, Paris)
Armour R M Ogorkiewicz (Stevens, London)
War as I knew it G S Patton (Houghton Mifflin, Boston)
Pre-War Plans and Preparations M S Watson (Dept of the US Army, Washington, DC)